KENNETH C. DAVIS
ILLUSTRATED BY MACHIYO KODAIRA

DON'T
KNOW
MUCH
ABOUT® **Martin Luther**
King Jr.

HarperCollinsPublishers

Amistad

Photo credits: Page 18, courtesy of the Martin Luther King, Jr. National Historic Site. All other photographs courtesy of the Library of Congress.

Amistad is an imprint of HarperCollins Publishers Inc.

This is a Don't Know Much About® book.

Don't Know Much About® is the trademark of Kenneth C. Davis.

Don't Know Much About® Martin Luther King Jr.

Library of Congress Cataloging-in-Publication Data

Davis, Kenneth C.

Don't know much about Martin Luther King Jr. / Kenneth C. Davis ; illustrated by Machiyo Kodaira.—1st ed.

p. cm.— (Don't know much about)

ISBN-10: 0-06-442129-5 (pbk.) — ISBN-10: 0-06-028822-1 (lib. bdg.)

ISBN-13: 978-0-06-442129-4 (pbk.) — ISBN-13: 978-0-06-028822-8 (lib. bdg.)

1. King, Martin Luther, Jr., 1929-1968—Juvenile literature. 2. African Americans— Biography—Juvenile literature. 3. Civil rights workers—United States—Biography—Juvenile literature. 4. Baptists—United States—Clergy—Biography—Juvenile literature. 5. African Americans—Civil rights—History—20th century—Juvenile literature. I. Kodaira, Machiyo, ill. II. Title. III. Series.

E185.97.K5D65 2006   2005007721

323'.092—dc22   CIP

                                                                                                        AC

Design by Charles Yuen
1 2 3 4 5 6 7 8 9 10
❖
First Edition

ACKNOWLEDGMENTS

An author's name goes on the cover of a book. But behind the book are a great many people who make it all happen. I would like to thank all the wonderful people at HarperCollins who helped make this book a reality, including Susan Katz, Kate Morgan Jackson, Barbara Lalicki, Martha Rago, Rosemary Brosnan, Amy Burton, Meredith Charpentier, Dana Hayward, Maggie Herold, Jeanne Hogle, and Rachel Orr. I would also like to thank David Black, Joy Tutela, and Alix Reid for their friendship, assistance, and great ideas. My wife, Joann, and my children, Jenny and Colin, are always a source of inspiration, joy, and support, and without them my work would not be possible.

I especially thank Robert Jackson, historical consultant, for reviewing the manuscript and providing helpful insights; Sarah Thomson for researching the photos; Machiyo Kodaira for her striking illustrations; and Judy Levin for her unique contribution.

CONTENTS

Martin Luther King Jr.

Wet do you dream about? Becoming a running back who scores all the touchdowns? Being a movie star on the cover of a magazine? Do you dream of becoming a doctor, an astronaut, or even president? Those are all good dreams to have.

But this is the story of a man with a very different kind of dream. Martin Luther King Jr. once said he dreamed of a day when his four black children could walk to school holding hands with white children. Sounds simple, doesn't it? But in 1963, when he told Americans about that dream in a famous speech he made in Washington, D.C., it seemed impossible— especially to the millions of African Americans who were treated like second-class citizens.

Even though his goals might have seemed unattainable, Dr. King continued to dream. He dreamed of a world in which the laws protected everyone, not just whites. He dreamed of a world in which poor people could hope for a better life. He inspired millions of other people to dream with him. In the end he died for that dream.

Who was Martin Luther King Jr.? And why does one man matter so much? What was so important about this boy who grew up to be a preacher? And why does a man who never served as president or led an army in battle have a holiday named in his honor?

Like all the Don't Know Much About® books, this biography tells a true story by asking questions. The questions in this book are not just about Dr. King, but also about a time in American history when people had to fight very hard to go to school, vote, buy a house, and hold a job—basic rights everyone deserves. They're also about how, even when laws change to guarantee that everyone has those rights, people's attitudes do not always change with them. Sometimes these questions are difficult to answer. But they're important to ask.

Don't Know Much About® biographies are about real people who did real things in real places. This is a story of how one brave leader didn't think that injustice and inequality were part of the American dream. "I have a dream that one day this nation will rise up and live out the true meaning of its creed," Dr. King once said. He fought his whole life making that dream come true. And the way in which he did it—not by going to war or running for political office—changed America and the world in a way that few people in history ever do.

I hope the story of Martin Luther King Jr.'s dream and the way he tried to make it come true helps you dream of great things too.

CHAPTER 1

Childhood in Sweet Auburn

King's birthplace

Who is Michael Luther King Jr.?

On January 15, 1929, Reverend King jumped so high with excitement that he hit the ceiling. His first son had just been born. He was named Michael Luther King Jr.

Yes, *Michael* Luther King. That was Reverend King's name, too. But in 1934 Reverend King went on a tour of Africa, Europe, and Palestine (the country that is now Israel), where he visited Jerusalem and other places in the Bible. When he came home, he changed his name and his son's name to Martin.

The name he chose suggests that he believed they were destined for great things: Martin Luther was the man who began the Protestant religion, separating from the Catholic church in the 1500s.

But even after his name change, Martin Luther King Jr. was mostly called M.L. or Little Mike.

What was M.L's family like?

His mother, Alberta Christine, was the daughter of a successful minister, the Reverend Adam Daniel Williams. Reverend Williams had become president of the Atlanta chapter of the National Association for the Advancement of Colored People (called the NAACP) soon after it was founded in 1909. When a local newspaper called NAACP members "dirty and ignorant," he organized a black boycott of the paper. That boycott put the newspaper out of business.

Alberta was the Williamses' only child. She was a shy girl, but smart—and a talented musician. Alberta was a graduate of Atlanta's Spelman College, a rare accomplishment in the days when very few people of any race went to college.

M.L.'s father had an entirely different upbringing. Mike King was the second of ten children born to sharecroppers in rural Georgia. His mother encouraged him to leave home at age fifteen to get away from poverty and from his father, who beat both him and his mother. So he plowed fields, worked in a tire plant, and preached at small churches.

When Mike King moved to Atlanta and met Alberta Williams, he knew right away that he wanted to marry her. His friends thought he was kidding. To marry the daughter of a successful minister, he'd have to stop sounding like an uneducated farmer's kid. So twenty-year-old Mike King went back to fifth grade, even though his legs were too big to fit under a desk.

After he finished high school, he applied to Morehouse College, where Reverend Williams had studied. He failed his entrance exams, but talked the school's registrar into admitting him anyway. And in 1926 he married Alberta Williams. The couple moved into the Williamses' house, and Mike King became Reverend Williams's assistant pastor.

By the time M.L. was born, his father and grandfather were the ministers of the richest church in the most important city in the South. After Reverend Williams died in 1931, Reverend Michael Luther King Senior (whom family and friends called "Daddy" King) became the minister of Ebenezer Baptist Church.

Reverend King assumed M.L. was next in line.

What was so "sweet" about "Sweet Auburn"?

The Kings lived at 501 Auburn Avenue in Atlanta, the capital of Georgia. At one end were black-owned businesses; at the other end were houses. The street was lined with trees that blossomed with sweet-smelling flowers such as magnolias and dogwoods. Many of the people who lived there were professionals, including teachers and business owners. Some people even had cars. Owning a car was a big deal in 1929. The black community of Atlanta was proud of their sweet Auburn Avenue.

Was the King family rich?

They weren't rich, but they had a lot of things that many people didn't have, including a car and a house with electricity and indoor plumbing.

When M.L. was growing up, many houses had electricity and indoor toilets, bathtubs, and running water, but most didn't. Martin Luther King's future wife, Coretta Scott, grew up at the same time but lived on a farm instead of in a city. The Scotts weren't poor, but her family still got water from a well and used an outhouse.

M.L. grew up in a house that looks old-fashioned to us. The kitchen did have a gas stove, but instead of a refrigerator it had an icebox with a big chunk of ice in it. After using the washing machine, someone had to feed wet clothes through a wringer one piece at a time and hang them outside to dry. The Kings' house also had central heating, and one of M.L.'s jobs was to bring coal from the shed in the backyard to the furnace in the basement.

The parlor held the piano and the Victrola (record player). The study was also used as the family room, where the Kings listened to the big wooden radio (television wasn't invented yet) and played board games. M.L.'s favorite game was Monopoly.

Even in this big house, M.L. and his younger brother, Alfred Daniel (called A.D.), shared a bedroom.

Christine, a year and a half older than M.L., had a room of her own. The extra rooms were for guests. Southern hotels were for whites only, so families— especially ministers' families—were used to having overnight visitors. M.L. and A.D. often slept on cots on the big hallway landing outside their room.

In 1941 Daddy King moved his family into a big brick house in an even more fashionable neighborhood. They weren't millionaires, but they had very comfortable lives without money worries, even after the Great Depression began and more than half of the city's blacks were on public relief. Martin Luther King later wrote about how guilty he felt as a child when he saw people lined up on the streets waiting for handouts of food. When he was grown up, he never wanted to live in a fancy house. And he never did.

THE GREAT DEPRESSION

America is really lucky. Most of the time, the economy is pretty good. That means people can find jobs and make a decent living. Families can eat well and buy the things they need and want. But sometimes the economy is not so good. Businesses close. When that happens and lots of people lose their jobs, it is called a *depression*.

In 1929 the Great Depression wiped out the banks and more jobs than ever before. By the early 1930s, one out of four workers had lost their jobs. A million Americans lived in shacks made of tar paper and old wooden boxes. Even some rich people lost their homes and moved to the "Hoovervilles"—temporary encampments that grew up at the edges of most cities. They were named for President Hoover, who people felt was not doing enough to solve the country's economic problems. It was a hard, hungry time.

When M.L. was a little boy, could people see that he was going to grow up to be special?

In many ways M.L. was just like any ordinary kid growing up in the 1930s. He liked baseball, kites, model airplanes, and bike riding. M.L. was small for his age and plump. (He wasn't especially handsome.) He loved the

> ### ATLANTA'S FAMOUS PRODUCT
>
> M.L.'s twenty-five-cents-a-week allowance was enough for five bottles of Atlanta's most famous product: Coca-Cola.

typical foods of a black southern childhood—fried chicken, barbeque, ham hocks, corn bread, and greens. He would love these foods his whole life.

M.L. was smart and he especially loved words. As a small child listening to a visiting preacher, he said, "I'm going to get me some of those big words someday." (He did, too, but he was never very good at spelling them.) His father said M.L. loved books before he could even read them. He also had a beautiful voice, and his mother liked to have him sing solos in church.

M.L. even got into trouble like an ordinary kid. Christine complained that he would hide in the bathroom when it was his turn to help wash dishes. Once he hit A.D. in the head with a telephone and knocked him out cold. There was also the day the King children decided to delay their piano lesson. They loosened the legs of the piano stool so when their teacher sat down, the stool crashed to the floor, piano teacher and all. Christine, M.L., and A.D. thought this was hilarious. Their father did not, and they were all whipped—a common punishment in

those days and one that Daddy King used often.

There were just a few things about M.L. that his family found unusual. For one thing, when his father whipped him, he wouldn't cry out loud, ever. He just looked so sad that his grandmother, who lived with them, cried instead. M.L. and his grandmother were very close to each other. One day when A.D. slid down the staircase banister (something both boys enjoyed), he knocked their grandmother unconscious. M.L. thought she was dead and that it was his own fault for not controlling his brother. So he jumped out a second-story window. Luckily M.L. and his grandmother were both fine, but his action is an example of how sensitively he felt about things.

How did M.L. learn about segregation?

About the time M.L. started school, his white friends—whose father's store was across the street from his house—weren't allowed to play with him anymore. Hurt and puzzled, he asked his mother what was wrong. She had to explain to him that he and his friends would go to different schools, drink from different water fountains, and use different public bathrooms. "You're just as good as anyone else," his mother said, as black parents said to their children all over the South. M.L. knew that was true, yet segregation meant that the Kings couldn't go to most restaurants or public parks. When M.L. went to a movie, he had to sit upstairs in the "colored" section. Being black meant he couldn't sit in the front of the bus or have a dish of ice cream at a lunch counter.

Drinks for white customers only

King's family had money, a beautiful house, education, and the respect of the black community. Yet segregation laws meant that M.L. didn't have the same rights as any white person.

"THE *N* WORD"

All insults are meant to hurt. "Nigger" is an especially mean one, because for many years blacks were unable to fight back. A person who objected to being called "nigger" was an "uppity nigger," and the "uppity niggers" could be *lynched*, or killed by individuals or mobs without legal sanction. The law said murder was illegal, but no southern jury would convict a white person of killing a black one.

Today many books and newspapers will not use the word "nigger," even in a quotation. It has become known as "the *N* word," the word too terrible even to write. But refusing to use the word doesn't change history. The word was once used, like a punch in the face, to black people all over the country. Most southern whites also addressed African-American adults by their first names or called them "boy" or "girl." Yet black adults had to say "yes, sir" or "yes, ma'am" even to white teenagers.

When Martin Luther King Jr. was growing up, the most polite word for an African American was "Negro."

What did M.L. learn from his family about how to deal with segregation?

He learned from his father to resist it whenever possible. One time he and his father walked out of a shoe store when the clerk tried to seat them in the back. M.L. remembered his father saying, "I don't care how long I have to live with this system, I will never accept it." Another time Reverend King talked back to a police officer who had pulled him over for speeding. When the trooper said, "Show me your license, boy," Reverend King pointed to M.L. and said, "This is a boy. I am a man." The startled trooper said that he needed to see his license anyway. Reverend King was lucky. The trooper could have yanked him out of his car and beaten him to death. Blacks were not allowed to talk back to whites. That wasn't a law, but it was the way things were.

Why couldn't Homer Plessy sit in the train seat he had a ticket for?

In 1891 a group of educated blacks in New Orleans, Louisiana, tried to get rid of the segregation laws. A man named Homer Plessy was arrested for sitting in the "white" part of a train. His lawyers argued that since blacks and whites had equal rights, no one should arrest Plessy for sitting in a seat he had paid for. The case went to the Supreme Court—the highest court in the United States.

The nine judges who make up the U.S. Supreme Court are supposed to decide if a law is fair or not, according to the Constitution. In 1896 the Supreme Court decided that there was nothing wrong with dividing races socially. They said that separate seats were okay as long as they were "separate but equal." But the truth is that the black seats and other segregated facilities such as schools were never equal for blacks. This Court decision opened the way for many laws that separated blacks and whites in America called "Jim Crow laws." By the time of M.L.'s childhood, these laws were common throughout the entire South.

CHAPTER 2

M.L. Grows Up

Ebenezer Baptist Church

What was M.L. like as he grew up?

His voice changed into the rich, deep voice for which he became famous. He remained a good student and excelled at sports, but he also loved to dance and to flirt. A.D. admired him, yet said he could never keep up with his big brother.

M.L. also became interested in clothes. He wore fashionable tweed suits, so his friends nicknamed him "Tweed" or "Tweedie." Later in his life, after he became a minister without much money, he still liked expensive suits.

When did M.L. begin to show what kind of person he would become?

When M.L. was twelve, he sneaked off to watch a parade when he was supposed to be doing his homework. By the time he got home, his grandmother had died of a heart attack. M.L. blamed himself. As he had done once before, he leaped out the window, sure her death was his fault. He didn't break any bones, but he was broken inside, crying and sleepless for many days.

His parents said his grandmother's death was God's will and not his fault, but M.L. wasn't comforted. Even though he seemed calm at her funeral, he often appeared calm on the outside. Pictures of him as a man show him looking steady and solemn even in times of great adversity. After his grandmother's death, M.L. felt confused as well as guilty. His parents said she was alive in heaven, but he wasn't sure. He began to question some of the things he was taught at his father's church. When M.L. was thirteen, he told his Sunday school class that he didn't believe Christ's body had risen from the dead. That was a shocking thing for him to say!

At fourteen M.L. had another experience that he would remember his entire life. Already an excellent public speaker, he traveled ninety miles with his teacher to Dublin, Georgia, to give a speech in a contest. His speech was called "The Negro and the Constitution"—a subject that would continue to interest him his whole life. On the way home, the white bus driver made M.L. and his teacher stand because white people wanted their seats. Then he cursed them because they didn't move fast enough.

M.L.wanted to refuse, but his teacher said they had to obey the law, and he didn't want to get her in trouble. "It was the angriest I have ever been in my life," he would write later.

When did he first encounter an integrated world?

The summer of 1944, after he graduated from high school, he went north to pick tobacco in Connecticut. Many southern kids worked in the fields near their homes picking cotton, but M.L.'s experience was different. He worked with an integrated group of black and white teenagers, many of them on their way to college. During their time off, they went into the nearby city of Hartford, where they could eat together in restaurants and sit together at the movies. M.L. found the whole experience "exhilarating." Yet he was shocked on the train ride home when, as they crossed into Virginia,

the conductor said he had to sit behind a curtain in the segregated dining car.

M.L. also wanted to know what work was like for ordinary black men in the South—men who wouldn't be able to go to college. So the next summer, he took jobs loading mattresses and carrying luggage. The work was hard, but harder still was being called names. He quit one job when a white boss called him a "nigger."

Why did M.L. go to college when he was only fifteen?

Because he had skipped three grades of school, and World War II had started. The military had scooped up so many students from Morehouse—the same college where M.L.'s father and grandfather had gone—that the leaders of the school discussed closing it until the war ended. Instead, college president Dr. Benjamin Mays decided to let twelfth graders in.

Was he a great student when he got to college?

Although M.L. was smart and had breezed through school, he had a hard time with his work at Morehouse. He was reading at an eighth-grade level, and his marks were only average. The segregated schools he had gone to had not given him a good education.

M.L. lived at home when he went to college, but he still managed to become a party animal. He loved to dance, flirt, and tell dirty jokes. Southern ministers-in-training were definitely not supposed to behave like that. Drinking, card playing, and smoking were all forbidden too. When Reverend King caught M.L. at a dance, he forced the seventeen-year-old to apologize in front of the whole church. M.L. was a lively, fun-loving guy. It would be hard for him when he became famous and had to be on his best behavior most of the time.

Still, he didn't spend all his time at college partying. He loved to read. One piece of literature he read and thought hard about was by Henry David Thoreau. In this famous essay, known today as "Civil Disobedience," Thoreau argues that sometimes a minority might have the power to change unjust laws through nonviolent resistance.

CIVIL DISOBEDIENCE (PART ONE)

In "Civil Disobedience," published in 1849, New Englander Henry David Thoreau explains why he refused to pay his taxes. The U.S. had begun a war with Mexico, and there were also new laws that made it illegal for northerners to help escaping slaves. Thoreau went to jail rather than pay taxes that would support government policies he believed were wrong.

AMERICAN VOICES

❝Under a government which imprisons any unjustly, the true place for a just man is also in prison. . . . A minority is powerless while it conforms to the majority . . . but it is irresistible when it clogs by its whole weight. If the alternative is to keep all just men in prison, or give up war and slavery, the State will not hesitate which to choose. ❞
—**Henry David Thoreau**, "Civil Disobedience," 1849

What did M.L. dream of doing after college?

He thought of becoming a medical doctor, but he wasn't great at science. He also considered being a lawyer, and made speeches to an imaginary jury in front of a mirror. M.L. wanted to change the laws that kept black people from voting, having rights, and maintaining dignity. He wanted to end segregation.

Why didn't M.L. want to become a minister?

He wanted to help people, but he didn't think being a minister was the best way to do that, even though that's what his father expected. When M.L. was growing up, very few black churches were working to change the political system. Even though Reverend King was a college graduate and a member of the NAACP, he didn't talk about the injustice of segregation in his sermons.

Black churches gave people hope for a time in the future—maybe in heaven—when their lives would be better, but most ministers didn't tell people to get out there and shake up the world. What church did do was give people a strong community where they felt safe, and the strength to go on with their hard lives. It made the world more bearable, but it didn't change it.

The church was a comfort to many people, but it wasn't comfortable to M.L. In fact, he found his

father's church to be embarrassing. Reverend King "walked the benches": He would come down from his pulpit and dance across the church pews, stepping over people while still preaching. This didn't suit M.L. at all. He was painfully aware of white stereotypes of black people. Blacks in movies or onstage weren't smart or educated, and they didn't have much self-control. They laughed too much and sang too loudly. That stereotype was the opposite of what M.L. wanted to be. Although he was lively and mischievous, he wanted people to recognize that he was also intelligent, educated, and dignified. There was no way M.L. was going to dance over the pews. The little boy who wanted big words had become a young man who was interested in big ideas. His father's church didn't encourage people to have big ideas. And that was the only kind of church he knew.

M.L. became a sociology major.

What did M.L. learn in college that made him change his mind about becoming a minister?

Even though he didn't get good grades, his college education would shape the way he thought for the rest of his life. By his senior year, he worked with an interracial council of students from different colleges. Meeting white college students helped him decrease his resentment of whites.

Several people at Morehouse also influenced him. English professor Gladstone Lewis Chandler loved words as much as M.L. did. He made big words into a game for his students, but he also taught them to think, write, and speak clearly.

George D. Kelsey, a religion professor, showed M.L. a way to read the Bible that was different from his father's fundamentalist approach. Kelsey said people didn't have to take everything in the Bible literally. They didn't have to believe, for example, that Jonah lived for three days in the belly of a whale. Kelsey taught that the Bible was full of other kinds of truths—important truths about how people should live and treat one another. A minister didn't have to preach just about people's souls and about how great heaven would be. He could also teach about injustice and social change. M.L. felt set free by these ideas. "The shackles of fundamentalism were removed from my body," he wrote later.

Finally the president of the college showed M.L. that a preacher could be something different from what his father and his father's friends were. Dr. Benjamin Mays was a minister out to change the world, and he wanted to educate students who would help. He was a member of the NAACP and spoke out about the hypocrisy of white churches that supported segregation.

M.L.'s teachers at Morehouse showed him that a minister was in a great position to help make big changes. The minister of a black church was well respected and listened to. He was the natural leader of his community.

And so M.L. decided to become a minister after all.

His happy father immediately made him an assistant pastor of Ebenezer Baptist Church and asked him to give a sermon. Eighteen-year-old M.L. used too many big words, but the congregation still thought he was great. Only he and his friends knew that he had borrowed the sermon from a book instead of writing it himself.

THE 1940S: RACE RELATIONS GET BETTER AND WORSE

World War II ended in 1945, while Martin Luther King was still in college. After the war black veterans came home in uniform. They had fought for America, and now they thought they would get respect. Instead they found that racists were angry at "uppity" black veterans. In 1946 six of them were lynched during a three-week period.

Yet there were signs of improvement for black Americans. In 1946 the Supreme Court ruled that segregation on interstate buses was unconstitutional. In 1947 Jackie Robinson joined the Brooklyn Dodgers, becoming the first black baseball player in the modern Major Leagues. And labor leader A. Philip Randolph began organizing a march to protest segregation in the military, which was desegregated the next year by President Harry S. Truman.

Why did King want to go to Crozer Theological Seminary?

By the time he graduated from college in 1948, his ideas were very different from his father's. King needed to get away from home and learn more before he could become the kind of minister he wanted to be—and not the kind his father expected. He didn't want to have to apologize when he went dancing. And he liked the idea of going to an integrated school and testing his mind against the minds of students of different races.

Crozer Theological Seminary was in Chester, Pennsylvania, a few miles south of Philadelphia. It was about the oddest place a black southern minister's son could have ended up. With fewer than one hundred students, Crozer was an experiment. Many colleges at the time wouldn't even let men and women study at the same school. Crozer admitted men, women, blacks, whites, Asians, Native Americans, and students from other countries.

King could barely have imagined a school where you could hear people playing pool downstairs while you practiced sermons. Card playing, drinking, smoking, dancing—the school *allowed* all these things. Crozer broke nearly every rule King had grown up with.

Did King like Crozer?

He had never been to an integrated school before. Even after working with whites in Connecticut and making white friends at the interracial council in college, he still worried about white stereotypes of blacks. He wanted to give off the best impression possible. So at first he was very stiff and formal. His room was neat and clean. He was always perfectly dressed and groomed, his clothes starched and ironed and his shoes polished. He would never be late for a class, and he wouldn't laugh out loud in public. He once scolded another black student for keeping beer in his room. The other student told him not to be a jerk. King was, he admitted later, "grimly serious for a time."

Although King didn't forget that he was a black man in an integrated community, he began to relax. His natural playfulness and enjoyment of a good time returned. He began to smoke (which he would do privately for the rest of his life) and became a good pool player. By the time King left Crozer, several young women believed they were engaged to him. But he didn't just use his years at Crozer to improve his flirting and pool-playing skills. He also became an excellent student, often surrounded by piles of books that he would read far into the night.

What was the biggest trouble King got into at Crozer?

He fell in love with a white woman, the daughter of one of the college cooks. After six months his friends persuaded him that an interracial marriage would ruin his chances of becoming a southern minister. King was unhappy and angry that society's rules could stop the marriage of two people who loved each other, but the couple agreed not to marry.

What did King study at Crozer?

He took nine classes on giving sermons. He was so good that other students would come to hear him. But a local minister who heard King give a practice sermon said that he sounded snobby. Too many big words, he complained.

King and his friend Walter McCall, who had been at Morehouse with him, used to play a game with sermons. First they would listen to a classmate give a practice sermon. Then McCall would give the same sermon using the emotional style of a southern black preacher and King would imitate how one of their Crozer teachers would speak on the same subject, in a very detached, intellectual way. Later King would become famous for his beautiful, dramatic speaking style, but he was like a Major League ballplayer: He had natural talent *and* he practiced.

King also studied philosophy and religion—all different religions—in order to discover what to believe about God and about human nature. He thought about whether people were basically good or basically evil. He continued to learn about the "social gospel," which was religion that addresses social and economic conditions. It didn't just tell people that they should trust in God and suffer patiently. It told them how to go out into the world and change it.

AMERICAN VOICES

❝ [King has] an attitude of aloofness, disdain, and possibly snobbishness which prevent his coming to close grips with the rank and file of ordinary people. Also a smugness that refuses to adapt itself to the demands of ministering effectively to the average Negro congregation. **

—**Reverend William E. Gardner**, evaluating King's practice sermon to his congregation

Did King leave Crozer with a plan for a Civil Rights movement?

At Morehouse King had read Thoreau's "Civil Disobedience." Now he learned about Mohandas Gandhi. Gandhi had read Thoreau too and had organized protests that led to India's independence from British rule in 1947. King doubted this could work in the United States. The Indian people were in the majority in India, while southern blacks were a minority in America.

Although King didn't leave Crozer with a plan for a nonviolent movement, his ideas about how to end segregation and violence against blacks had changed a great deal. When he came to Crozer, he had believed that an armed rebellion might be necessary before blacks would have equal rights in the United States. Now he rejected violence. He had read Thoreau and Gandhi, but he had also considered what the Bible said and decided that perhaps his grandmother and mother were right: Maybe loving your enemies could somehow be a way to change how whites treated blacks.

In 1951 King graduated from Crozer Theological Seminary at the top of his class, as a thoughtful, popular, and well-educated twenty-two-year-old.

CIVIL DISOBEDIENCE (PART TWO)

Mohandas "Mahatma" Gandhi

Mohandas Gandhi was a Hindu born in India in 1869. He went to London, England, to study law when he was nineteen. While he was there, he read Thoreau's "Civil Disobedience" and later began to apply Thoreau's ideas to the freeing of India from British rule. He was jailed numerous times for leading boycotts. In 1930 Gandhi led a famous protest in which thousands of Indians marched two hundred miles to the sea to get salt, defying the law that said they must buy taxed salt from the British. Finally, in 1947, India won its independence from Britain.

Millions of people called Gandhi "Mahatma," which means "Great Soul." However, not everyone appreciated his hard work. Gandhi was assassinated in 1948 by a Hindu who was angry at Gandhi's efforts to make peace between Hindus and Muslims. People all over the world mourned his death.

What kind of doctor was Dr. Martin Luther King?

Not the kind who cures sore throats.

After King graduated from Crozer, his father expected him to come home and—finally—be his assistant minister for good. But King still didn't want to work with his father. Also, he wanted the title "Doctor" in front of his name before he went back down south, where white people wouldn't even call a black man "Mister." He wanted respect.

So he went to Boston University to get his doctorate, the most advanced college degree. Often a person with a doctorate goes on to teach at a university. That worried King's father. He wanted an assistant minister, not a college professor. But still, he gave in, as he so often did to his older son.

Daddy King sent M.L. off to Boston University with a new green Chevrolet.

What did King do in Boston besides study?

He met his future wife, Coretta Scott. She was the daughter of a farmer from Alabama and had worked hard to prepare herself to become a professional singer of classical music. This was a difficult career for anyone to achieve, but especially for a black woman with no money in the early 1950s.

When M.L. first met Coretta, he thought she had character, intelligence, personality, and beauty. She thought he was short. (He *was* short—only about five feet six inches tall.) But then, as he spoke, he seemed to grow taller and better looking. Would Coretta give up her dream of being a professional singer to marry this man? She would have to. King was very clear that he needed a traditional minister's wife, a woman who would be patient with his congregation and take care of the children. But Coretta Scott was also smart and independent, and although she did give up her plans to be a concert singer, she still sang in public.

King's father didn't approve of the match. He wanted his son to marry a girl from a good family in Atlanta. He even had one picked out. But when M.L. made it known that he definitely intended to marry Coretta, his father gave in.

On June 18, 1953, they were married at the Scotts' house in Marion, Alabama. Coretta wanted a small, simple wedding. She wore a long pale-blue dress instead of a formal white bridal gown, and she had cooked most of the food for the reception herself. By the time the King family (and their friends from

Atlanta and some deacons and trustees of Ebenezer Baptist Church) arrived, it wasn't as small as she had wanted, but they still got married in her parents' garden. Although her parents were living in a nicer house than the one she'd grown up in, she'd worried that the Kings would find her family very "countrified." Her worry was unnecessary, because the families liked each other just fine.

Before the wedding King had driven from Boston to Atlanta and then from Atlanta to Marion. By the time the reception was over, he was so tired that the new Mrs. King had to drive them to the place where they would spend their wedding night: a guest room at a funeral parlor owned by friends of the Scotts. Hotels didn't take black guests.

MARTIN LUTHER KING ON ROLLER SKATES

The summer Martin and Coretta got married, Coretta's mother came to Boston to visit. One Sunday, after King had preached a very serious sermon, they all went to the amusement park. King rode the roller coaster and the Ferris wheel and roller-skated, acting as silly as a four-year-old, said Mrs. Scott.

CHAPTER 3

"Don't Ride the Buses on Monday"

King speaks at a mass meeting in Montgomery.

How did King get his job as minister of Dexter Avenue Baptist Church?

After the Kings got married, Martin still had to complete some work at Boston University and Coretta had to finish her musical education. (She changed her major from performance to teaching.) She had such a demanding schedule that King did a lot of the housework. He was a good cook. Then, in 1954, he found a job as a minister—not in Atlanta (to his father's annoyance) or in the North (to his wife's sorrow, since she had liked living in the North), but in Montgomery, Alabama.

Montgomery had been the first capital of the Confederacy during the Civil War. When the Kings moved there, it was a city of about 120,000 people. Most of the 50,000 black citizens were poor. Most of the people in King's congregation at Dexter Avenue Baptist Church were not. Many members were educated and middle class. They were teachers, doctors, or business owners at a time when black people couldn't be hired to do most jobs.

Dexter's congregation had been proud of its previous minister, Dr. Vernon Johns, who spoke six or seven languages, including ancient Greek. But he had also caused a lot of embarrassment. He believed that the congregation looked down on people who hadn't accomplished much, especially people like farmers who worked in the dirt. So Dr. Johns would bring vegetables he had grown (and some dirt) and sell them outside the church, right where everyone—blacks *and* whites—could see. The congregation fired him.

It wanted a smart, educated minister who wouldn't embarrass them. Martin Luther King certainly seemed to be that. He was such a nice young man, newly married and from a well-known family in Atlanta. Surely he wouldn't cause any problems.

66 You mean that little boy is my pastor? He looks like he ought to be home with his mamma. 99
—**Professor Mary Fair Burks**, Alabama State College, 1954

What did King do his first year and a half in Montgomery?

The Kings settled in at the parsonage, the small, white-painted house where the church's minister lived. Martin joined the NAACP. He got up before 6 A.M. every morning to write. He wouldn't be "Doctor" King until he completed a book-length essay called a dissertation, which he finished in the spring of 1955.

On November 17, 1955, King became the father of a baby named Yolanda Denise, called "Yoki" for short. (The fancy name was Coretta's idea. King wanted their next daughter to be called something simpler.)

Even though he was a new father, he still made plenty of time for his reading and writing. He proudly told his congregation that he had read 26 books and 102 magazines his first year as minister. He worked hard on his sermons, taking fifteen hours to write out every word and then learn them by heart so he wouldn't need his notes. (He liked to set the notes aside as he began to speak—just to show that he didn't need them.)

King also began to meet more people. Early on, he met the Reverend Ralph Abernathy, who had been preaching against segregation since 1952, when he'd first had a pulpit to preach from. King liked him right away. Some people called them "Mr. Rough and Mr. Smooth," because Abernathy was a gruff, funny man and King was so polite and polished. Nevertheless, they quickly became the closest of friends.

RALPH ABERNATHY: "MR. ROUGH"

King and Abernathy

Growing up in rural Alabama, Ralph Abernathy was one of twelve children of a sharecropper. Still, his was not an ordinary sharecropping family, because his father was able to save money and buy his own land, which was no easy task.

Abernathy was educated in southern schools. He never had—or seemed to want—King's polish. Yet the two remained close until King's death, telling jokes and making each other laugh. Perhaps with Abernathy, King was most able to show the part of himself that had loved to have fun, even after outsiders knew him only as the powerful and serious Reverend Dr. Martin Luther King Jr.

At various times Abernathy became jealous of King, feeling that his own role in the Civil Rights movement was getting very little notice. Still, Abernathy moved his family from Montgomery to Atlanta in 1961 to work more closely with King, who was living there at the time. When King went to jail, it was generally Abernathy who went with him. After King's death in 1968, Abernathy helped to carry out many of King's plans for the Civil Rights movement.

What action is considered the beginning of the modern Civil Rights movement?

Rosa Parks, a forty-two-year-old seamstress and Civil Rights activist, refused to give up her seat to a white man on a Montgomery city bus on Thursday, December 1, 1955. When the driver told her that he'd have her arrested, she said, "You may do that." He did. The next day Rosa Parks was found guilty of breaking the segregation laws.

Why was sitting in the back of a bus a big deal?

For most of Montgomery's black citizens, riding the bus was a daily humiliation. Blacks made up about 75 percent of the riders on the buses, because more whites had cars. But the front ten rows of seats were for whites, and even if there wasn't a single white passenger on the bus, blacks couldn't sit there. Blacks had to ride buses to work or to shop downtown—and every time, they were reminded that they were second-class citizens. Many drivers made black passengers pay their money, then get off the bus and reenter through the back door. Some would speed off before the passenger could get back on. They called black women "cows" and "apes," and sometimes hit blacks who didn't do what they wanted. Some drivers even carried guns.

What happened after Rosa Parks was arrested?

Various black groups that had been waiting for a chance to challenge bus segregation leaped into action. Although other people had been arrested for refusing to give up their seats, Montgomery's black leaders had been waiting for someone like Rosa Parks: a woman of dignity with a good reputation, who would not resist arrest or disturb the peace.

The Women's Political Council (WPC), an organization of black middle-class women, had been eager to boycott the bus company. E. D. Nixon, the founder of the Montgomery NAACP, and some other NAACP workers had been wanting to sue the bus company. He wanted them to desegregate. When Nixon found out that Rosa Parks had been arrested, he crowed, "This is the case! This is the case!" And Alabama State College professor Jo Ann Robinson, president of the WPC, stayed up all night mimeographing leaflets. The leaflets told blacks not to ride the buses on Monday.

1954: TV DINNERS AND CIVIL RIGHTS

The year the Kings moved to Montgomery, the microchip and the TV dinner were invented—and the U.S. Supreme Court decided the most important law case of the century. It was called *Brown v. Board of Education*.

Seven-year-old Linda Brown took a long trip to school every day because she couldn't go to the white school near her house. Her father sued the Board of Education of Topeka, Kansas. Then in Virginia, Barbara Johns, the sixteen-year-old niece of Vernon Johns, got all her classmates to strike in protest of the bad condition of their high school. These cases, along with several others, went together to the Supreme Court. The court finally decided—unanimously—that separate schools could never be equal, because segregating black children made them feel unequal.

Brown v. Board of Education gave people great hope that other segregated facilities would soon be declared unconstitutional.

Did people ride the buses on Monday?

King had worried. Everyone had worried. Suppose it rained on Monday? Suppose people wouldn't walk miles and miles to work? A lot of blacks were discouraged and afraid.

King was up early Monday morning, drinking coffee. He hadn't slept well. All of a sudden, he heard his wife calling, "Darling, it's empty!" She was pointing to a bus going by their house, one that was usually packed with blacks going to work. Fifteen minutes later another empty bus went by. Then another. In amazement King drove around the city looking at the buses. He saw only about eight black riders. The boycott was nearly a 100 percent success.

How did King become a president?

On Monday, December 5, there was a daytime meeting of black ministers and community leaders. Although they thought the boycott would just last a few days, they formed a new organization called the Montgomery Improvement Association (MIA) to run it. Never before had there been an organization that all Montgomery blacks could belong to. Although segregation laws didn't recognize the difference between a black bricklayer and a black college professor, the bricklayer and the professor did. E. D. Nixon felt that the NAACP looked down on him because he wasn't educated enough. The different groups of people working for desegregation often didn't get along. But everyone was going to have to band together—or else the boycott wouldn't work.

Martin Luther King Jr. wasn't part of any of these old disagreements about who could belong to what organization. Most people didn't even know who he was, but the people who knew him liked him. Also, some of the leaders were afraid they'd get in trouble with the segregationists of Montgomery. They were glad to have King, still new and an outsider, to take the blame.

What happened on Monday night?

The MIA planned to hold a mass meeting at the Holt Street Baptist Church at 7 P.M., so people could decide if they wanted to continue boycotting the buses. King and Abernathy were surprised by all the traffic on the way to the church. As they got closer, they could see what was causing it. It was only five o'clock, but the church was already overflowing. More than one thousand people filled the church, and about four thousand others spilled out into the streets. Cars were parked on the sidewalks and lawns. Loudspeakers were set up so that the people outside could hear. "This could turn into something big," said King in awe.

It *was* big. All those people, worn down by years of bad treatment, had never before believed they could make a difference. Now they were ready to protest.

Who spoke at the meeting?

The meeting began with hymns and prayers. Nixon and some ministers spoke.

Then King began his address. It wasn't like any speech he had ever given. Instead of having fifteen hours to prepare, he'd only had twenty minutes to scribble some notes. He had to speak from his heart. As he talked, he fell into the rhythms of his father's sermons, so that people became excited and started shouting "Amen!" and "That's right!" King said what was most important to them: They were tired of being kicked around, tired of oppression, tired of being segregated and humiliated. But King said also that if they would "protest courageously, and yet with Christian love . . . the historians will have to pause and say, 'There lived a great people—a black people—who injected new meaning and dignity into the veins of civilization.'"

People stood up, cheering and clapping for more than fifteen minutes.

❝I don't know what that boy is talkin' about, but I sure like the way he sounds.❞
—A woman who heard King speak during the meeting, as quoted by Abernathy in Stephen B. Oates's *Let the Trumpet Sound: The Life of Martin Luther King, Jr.*

❝When I hears Dr. King, I see angels' wings flying around his head.❞
—Another woman who heard King preach

What did the blacks of Montgomery want?

Segregation was a state law, so the bus company couldn't change it. A court case would have to challenge bus segregation. But the MIA would still demand some changes before blacks would ride the buses again.

After King spoke, Reverend Abernathy read the list of demands that the MIA would present to the bus company:

1. Drivers must treat passengers politely.

2. Blacks must not be asked to give up their seats to whites, but blacks would first fill the seats in the back of the bus, and whites would sit in the front.

3. The bus company must hire some black drivers.

Why was Montgomery nicknamed "The Walking City"?

Because the bus company and the city council said no to all the MIA's demands.

45

So people walked. And walked. And *walked.* They got tired and they wore out their shoes, but they were proud to walk. People sometimes turned down free rides. They wanted others to *see* them walk, to *see* them protest. "I'd crawl on my knees before I'd get back on them buses," said one domestic worker.

Other people rode bicycles. Or mules. Some white women who employed black maids or cooks threatened to fire them if they didn't ride the buses. "I told her to keep her money," reported one woman who was threatened by her boss. Other white women gave their black employees rides or gave them money for the MIA. Some whites even joined the boycott.

The MIA kept developing new ways to transport people, and the city kept shutting them down.

Black cab companies had agreed at the beginning of the boycott to charge ten cents (the price of a bus fare), instead of their usual forty-five cents. City officials arrested them for offering illegally low fares.

Black people (and some whites) volunteered their automobiles for use in car pools, and riders would pay fifteen cents for gas. King had gotten this idea from a minister who had been involved with the ten-day Baton Rouge bus boycott in June 1953. Still, the lending of cars was revolutionary. Few black people could afford them. Now others were letting their cars be driven by volunteers, including King. The police said that this use of private cars was an illegal taxi service.

Finally the MIA created a free public transportation system. People lent cars without charging gas money, and the churches bought station wagons. The MIA made a schedule of pickup and drop-off times and places all over the city.

The police would pull over drivers for ridiculous violations such as stopping too long at a stop sign. King was arrested for going thirty miles an hour in a twenty-five-mile-an-hour zone. That was his first arrest, and he was terrified. He was sure he would be taken from jail and lynched. Instead the head jailer, frightened by the crowd gathering outside in protest, was forced to free King. The car-pool system kept rolling.

The city was amazed—and furious—at how well the system worked. The bus company was losing money so fast that it might have to go out of business.

AMERICAN VOICES

❝Ain't gonna ride them buses no more,

Ain't gonna ride no more.

Why don't all the white folks know

That I ain't gonna ride no more.**❞**
                    —A song sung by Montgomery bus boycotters

> **❝** Here is one white ex–bus rider who would like to declare that as long as the boycott is on, it will be a dreary, rainy day, when I have a sprained ankle, and less than 45¢ cab fare, before I board one of those yellow rolling cell blocks again. **❞**
> —Letter to the editor of the *Montgomery Advertiser*

Was Martin Luther King frightened by the threats against his life?

King and the other people working on the boycott were threatened constantly. People would phone their houses at all hours, calling them names and telling them they would be killed. King told reporters that the protest was so important, it was worth risking his life for. But other times he said that he *was* afraid. He was a young man with a wife and a newborn baby. As he admitted to a friend from Crozer, there were days when he just couldn't believe what he had gotten himself into.

One day in January, King was so frightened that he cried. He had just gotten a threatening phone call: "If you aren't out of this town in three days, we gonna blow your brains out and blow up your house." Sitting at his kitchen table, King asked God for help. He asked God to make him strong and to tell him what to do. Later he said that he heard an "inner voice" tell him, "Stand up for righteousness. Stand up for justice. Stand up for truth." His fear left him. He called it his "kitchen table conversion"—the moment when he came to experience God in a new way. Even though he was a minister, King said that he had never felt God's presence like that before. He had become a minister because his father expected it and because it seemed like a good way to help people. Now he was filled with a new sense of courage.

Three days later he was speaking at an MIA meeting when someone rushed in with the news that King's house had been bombed. When he arrived home, he saw that his front porch and front window had been destroyed by dynamite. Several hundred people were waiting at his house, ready to defend King. Many of them were armed. The police commissioner and the mayor were there too, nervously promising to catch whoever had thrown the dynamite. The crowd was not impressed with this promise. The nonviolent Civil Rights movement was moments from ending in a riot.

King had already checked to make sure that his wife and daughter were safe. (When Coretta had heard the *thump* of the bomb on the porch, she had rushed to the nursery at the back of the house to get Yoki.) King spoke to the crowd; it was one of the many times in the fight for Civil Rights that he would calm people who were angry to the point of violence. King said there must be no violence, no revenge. "We must meet hate with love," he explained. "If I am stopped, our work will not stop. For what we are doing is right. What we are doing is just."

The crowd went home peacefully.

Why did King want them to be peaceful?

King said that white people who had been taught to hate were also victims. Desegregation was meant to make Montgomery better for *all* people. King wanted the protestors to boycott peacefully. He not only wanted them to refrain from fighting, but to behave so well that segregationists would feel ashamed of their own hatred.

As he had with the Crozer student who threatened him with a gun, King hoped to turn enemies into friends. He didn't just want to end segregation on buses. He wanted blacks and whites to live together in peace.

Did Coretta Scott King think her husband should stop taking risks with their lives?

No. But her father and Martin's father turned up the night of the bombing to persuade them to leave Montgomery—or at least to have Martin stop leading the protest. "It's better to be a live dog than a dead lion," said Daddy King. They refused. Coretta Scott King would not leave her husband or tell him he should stop working for a cause they both believed in.

King's parents never stopped worrying about him after that.

Did King's request for peace actually keep the peace?

The MIA responded to the bombing with legal action, not violence. Fred Gray, the young, black

Montgomery lawyer who was helping the boycotters, filed a lawsuit on January 31, 1956. It said that bus segregation was unconstitutional.

Segregationists reacted to the news of the lawsuit with even more violence. Ten thousand people attended a white supremacy rally in Montgomery, bragging that they'd give blacks a "whipping." One black neighborhood was bombed so often that it was nicknamed "Dynamite Hill." Segregationists threw rotten eggs and bricks at black people walking. Peace was still far from a reality.

How did the whites identify King as the boycott's leader?

Segregationists had always said that "their" Negroes were happy with being separate. The bus boycott showed this was nonsense, and it raised a big question: How had those "happy" black people (who whites also thought were stupid) ever organized something as huge and successful as the boycott? White newspapers like the *Montgomery Advertiser* looked for explanations. Maybe the NAACP was running it? No, the national NAACP didn't even support the boycott. They wanted segregation fought in the courts, not in the streets.

But what about this young minister with his big words and his northern education? Older ministers respected him. He had admitted to a reporter that he believed in integration. And he was an outsider, from Atlanta. The *Montgomery Advertiser* concluded, "Who is the acknowledged boycott leader? He seems to be the Reverend Martin Luther King, Jr."

Was King really the leader of the boycott?

On February 21 the city accused 115 people (including King, Parks, Abernathy, Nixon, and twenty-four ministers) of breaking an old law that made boycotts illegal. Black people had always been afraid and ashamed of being arrested. But now they were so angry that they put on their best clothes and went to the courthouse themselves. Altogether, 87 people were arrested.

Deciding to start with the movement's "leader," the court put King on trial first. His testimony was clear and forthright; he was proud to be convicted of trying to help his people. The court later questioned Claudette Colvin, a high-school student who had been arrested before Rosa Parks for refusing to give up her seat on a bus. When asked who the movement's leader was, Claudette answered, "The leaders are just we ourselves."

❝ The amazing thing about our movement is that it is a protest of the people. It is not a one man show. It is not the preachers' show. It is the people. The masses of people, who are tired of being trampled on, are responsible. The leaders couldn't stop it if they wanted to. ❞

—**Professor Jo Ann Robinson**, founder of the WPC, speaking to a black reporter about the bus boycott

How did people feel about King's leadership?

In truth, the boycott had been started by the WPC with Nixon's support, but neither would get the fame—or blame—that King got. The MIA treated Rosa Parks as a "symbol" of the boycott, not recognizing her many years of work for Civil Rights. And the boycott was kept going by ordinary people who walked to work every day and by all the volunteers who kept the carpool going. Yet it was King who spoke endlessly, raising money, lifting people's spirits, and reminding them of why they had to keep walking and protesting peacefully.

Many people followed and loved King—especially after his trial. But others were angry that King got the credit for other people's hard work.

The court found King guilty and fined him five hundred dollars or 386 days of hard labor. This made King—and the boycott—headline news around the country. Thousands of dollars of contributions poured in. The city was so embarrassed that it dropped all the other cases. Many white people were glad. The boycott was bad for business. Besides, people were ashamed that their city was behaving badly in front of the whole world.

King and the other Civil Rights workers would later learn to use news coverage as a powerful tool in their campaigns.

Who came to help Martin Luther King learn about running a nonviolent protest?

The court conviction made King even more famous. He was on TV and in all the newspapers. People compared him to Gandhi. They compared him to Moses, the Biblical prophet who led the Jews from

 slavery in Egypt to "the Promised Land." Some of the women called him "L.L.J."—Little Lord Jesus. He was getting more attention than he knew what to do with.

It was true that he had spoken of passive resistance and the power of love, but he had no experience of political organization. "I have no idea where this movement is going," he admitted to a friend.

People who weren't as well known as King had been staging nonviolent protests for years. Bayard Rustin, who had gone on interstate bus protests in 1947, came to Montgomery to help with the movement. He told King to get the guns out of his house and get rid of the armed guards outside. King said that he had to protect his family. Rustin said no. A nonviolent movement could never use violence, not even in self-defense. King suggested that maybe, if a few white people got hurt, the federal government would step in and enforce desegregation.

Years later Rustin said that to truly honor Dr. King, we must understand that he was *not* prepared to run this protest. King was learning as he went along. And he did get rid of the guns and armed guards.

Rustin also introduced King to a wealthy New York lawyer named Stanley Levison, a Civil Rights supporter who raised and donated money for the movement. Levison became one of King's closest advisers and lifelong friends.

The Reverend Glenn E. Smiley, a white southern minister who worked for a nonviolent protest group called the Fellowship of Reconciliation, taught King more about Gandhi. Although King had read about him in college, he didn't yet know how to conduct protests like Gandhi's. Some of Gandhi's methods, such as having people be arrested until the jails were full, would not be used until later Civil Rights protests.

However inexperienced King was, he got people to agree that nonviolence was necessary as a political tool. Even Nixon, who had little use for religion and wasn't a very peaceful person, knew that violent black protesters would have been lynched.

How did the bus boycott end?

On November 13, 1956, the Alabama State Court was about to rule that the carpool was an illegal transportation system. But just before they tried to shut it down, a reporter came into the court and  handed King a message: The United States Supreme Court had ruled 9 to 0 in favor of the protesters. On December 20 the Supreme Court delivered to the city of Montgomery its written order to desegregate the buses. After 381 days, the protesters had won.

What happened after the Supreme Court ruling?

King and Smiley sit together on an integrated bus.

More than eight thousand people held mass meetings of celebration in two black churches. King and Reverend Smiley got on the first integrated bus and posed together in the front for reporters.

As with many later Civil Rights victories, this one was followed by violence. Segregationists bombed black churches and the homes of MIA ministers. They shot out the Kings' front door and tried to blow up their whole house, but the bomb didn't go off. They shot at buses and at black passengers. For a time the city refused to run the buses at all.

King felt guilty about the violence. He told his congregation he hoped no one would have to die as a result of the struggle for freedom in Montgomery: "Certainly I don't want to die," he said. "But if anyone has to die, let it be me." King never stopped believing that the Civil Rights movement would cause him to be killed.

By the end of January, integrated buses were running on schedule. Some people said the Montgomery bus boycott was the nonviolent protest movement's first major victory. Others said it wasn't. The court changed the laws, said the NAACP. The protests didn't change them. Yet the whole country had seen that ordinary people protesting peacefully had made a difference. Other cities were having bus boycotts. And the blacks of Montgomery could hold their heads up proudly. They hadn't just been given the victory by the court. They had earned it.

CHAPTER 4

A Tough Job Ahead

First sit-in at Woolworth's lunch counter

Why was King so worried after the success of the Montgomery bus boycott?

He said he had a tough job ahead. King was only twenty-seven years old, but he was already famous. "People will be expecting me to pull rabbits out of the hat for the rest of my life," he told a reporter for the *New York Post* in April 1957.

And everyone would always be watching him. The young man who had loved to party, drink, smoke, play pool—no one but his closest friends would ever see that side of him again. He felt there were two Martin Luther Kings—the public leader that people looked up to, and the private person, a young man who got up every morning, drank his coffee, played with his baby, and tried to figure out what to do next.

Why did Martin Luther King want to form a new Civil Rights organization?

The NAACP wanted to change laws through legal battles, but even when it won, states sometimes ignored the court rulings. In any case, Alabama and other southern states had outlawed the NAACP in June 1956. Even if they hadn't, King believed that "legislation and court orders can only declare rights. They can never thoroughly deliver them. Only when the people themselves begin to act are rights on paper given life blood." He knew that the two main goals of the Civil Rights movement—voter registration and an end to segregation—needed to be achieved at least in part by community action.

The Montgomery movement had shown how well the churches could work to organize people. And so in January 1957, a group of ministers and other black leaders met in Atlanta. They would become the Southern Christian Leadership Conference (SCLC). King was elected president with little debate.

There were more than sixty people in the organization, but the group that became close friends and coworkers with King was small. They were an unusual crowd, but, as minister Andrew Young remarked, "Normal people don't challenge the laws of the land." Later, as they traveled around the South planning strategy, they would sit in their underwear (there was no air-conditioning in those days), drinking beer and nearly always disagreeing with one another. They would yell and argue and sometimes even throw chairs. King would stay calm, listening to everyone's opinions, and wait until he understood what should be done.

ANDREW YOUNG: VALUABLE LEADER

Andrew Young was born in New Orleans, Louisiana. He was the son of a dentist, but his father's middle-class job did not protect him from racism. His grandmother told him, "If anyone calls you a nigger and you don't hit him, don't come home unless you want a spanking." He didn't get many spankings.

Young went to Howard University, an all-black college in Washington, D.C., known for turning out well-educated professionals. Then he went to Hartford Theological Seminary in Connecticut. Like many of the people who would become involved in the Civil Rights movement, he studied the work of Gandhi.

Young worked for the National Council of Churches in New York City, but he later moved to Atlanta and began working with an SCLC voter registration program. His intelligence, steady calmness, and good sense of humor made him especially valuable to King and to the movement. Young continued to fight for Civil Rights after King's death and eventually became a representative to both Congress and the United Nations.

What was the first "Prayer Pilgrimage for Freedom" praying for?

One of the SCLC's first demonstrations was in Washington, D.C., on May 17, 1957, the third anniversary of *Brown v. Board of Education*. About twenty-five thousand people, black and white, marched—and prayed—for the right to vote.

Although others had organized the march, King's speech got the most attention. "Give us the ballot," he shouted. "Give us the ballot," the crowd shouted back. The *New York Amsterdam News* said of King, "The people will follow him anywhere." The SCLC's first campaign would be to try to register voters all across the South.

Why was voting so important?

Voting is one of the basic rights guaranteed to American citizens. As Abraham Lincoln declared in his 1863 Gettysburg Address, we have a government elected "of the people, by the people, for the people." That's why the United States is a democracy. The Fifteenth Amendment, added to the Constitution in 1870 after the Civil War, guaranteed this right to black men. But before people could vote, they had to register, or sign up. The southern states made it impossible for blacks to register. One African American from South Carolina memorized the whole Consitution but was not allowed to register because the person testing him insisted that he recite it in Chinese. There was even a black teacher who had to help a white official read the literacy test to her. He failed her anyway.

Without the vote, blacks couldn't be represented in government. Even in towns or cities where there were more blacks than whites, blacks couldn't elect people who would change the segregation laws. They couldn't elect judges or the people who appoint judges. And with the right to vote comes the right—and responsibility—of sitting on juries. All-white juries were one of the reasons a black person could hardly ever get justice in a southern courtroom. In 1958 a black man in Mississippi was given the death penalty for stealing less than two dollars.

Southern blacks were threatened, harassed, and even killed for trying to register to vote.

“ My father was a slave, and when he was freed, bought property and paid taxes. I have paid taxes for twenty-five years. I've never been arrested or in any kind of trouble. I sort of feel that as a citizen, I ought to have the right to vote. **”**
> —**Reverend C. M. Eiland**, a Mississippi minister, as quoted in Jack H. Pollard's "Literacy Tests," *American Mercury*, May 1947

When did King first visit a foreign country?

In September 1957 Martin and Coretta King were invited to the African country of Ghana to celebrate its independence from Great Britain. Between 1957 and 1961, more than twenty African nations would free themselves from white rule. King and many others believed the struggles of Africans against colonialism and of African Americans against segregation seemed connected. In both cases, black people were demanding their rights.

Who were the "Little Rock Nine"?

Big news was happening at home while King was out of the country. A federal court ordered Arkansas's governor, Orval Faubus, to integrate several schools, including Little Rock's Central High School. (The Little Rock schools were defying the Supreme Court's landmark decisions to end school segregation. These were a series of rulings beginning with the *Brown v. Board of Education* decision in 1954 that declared that the "separate but equal" concept was unconstitutional. Many other white schools had simply closed, rather than let blacks in.)

Instead of integrating, the governor called in the Arkansas National Guard to keep nine black students out. When the nine students reported to school on September 4, 1957, they were met by a screaming mob supported by guards in battle gear, carrying bayonets. The courts again ordered Faubus to allow the integration of the school.

The governor then withdrew the guards, leaving the students to a mob. "I hope they drag nine dead niggers out," someone screamed. That day the students had to be removed from the school for their own safety.

The taunts, hatred, and signs that said "Keep our schools white" were reported by the international news. President Dwight D. Eisenhower believed in integration but hadn't wanted to get involved, because he wanted whites in the South to vote for him. However, Arkansas's rebellion against the federal government could not be ignored. He sent in federal troops, saying, "Thus will be restored the image of America and all its parts, as one nation, indivisible, with liberty and justice for all."

On September 25 a van carried the nine students to the school. Jeeps armed with machine guns surrounded it. National Guardsmen were assigned to protect the students all year. The nine were spat on, kicked, cut with bottles, and called names; when one black girl finally dumped her chili on a white boy's head, *she* was suspended. But Central High was finally integrated—and stayed integrated.

Where was the Civil Rights movement moving?

The Civil Rights movement's biggest victory since the Montgomery bus boycott was the integration of Little Rock's Central High. King hadn't been responsible for its success, although one member of the SCLC, Daisy Bates, had helped to organize the integration.

King said he didn't know where the movement was going, let alone where *he* was going. Between 1957 and 1958, King traveled everywhere, giving more than two hundred speeches. Sometimes he would give more than four speeches a day. He would be on the road for the rest of his life. (He said he could tell what airport he was in by its smell.) King raised money for voter registration drives, to pay staff and lawyers, and, later, to bail people out of jail. And he spoke as he had in Montgomery, giving people hope, telling them that oppression could end and that justice was possible. People listened and cheered, yet there was no great action like the one in Montgomery.

One of the many places King went was to the White House. On June 23, 1958, President Eisenhower met with King, NAACP president Roy Wilkins, A. Philip Randolph, and another black leader named Lester B. Granger. These men urged the president to enforce *Brown v. Board of Education* in other schools, to encourage Congress to pass stronger Civil Rights laws, and to send federal officials to help register blacks to vote. King was disappointed in the meeting. He felt that the president had not promised to help them.

IT'S A BOY!

On October 23, 1957, Martin Luther King III was born. This time it was Coretta Scott King who objected to the name. She worried that it would be too hard for the boy to live up to his famous father. The boy was nicknamed Marty.

When Marty was born, Martin Luther King was away at a meeting. Coretta had to get used to his being away most of the time—as well as to his turning up unexpectedly with hungry coworkers.

How did Dr. King get a cross-shaped scar on his chest?

King—with help from Rustin and Levison—had written a book about the Montgomery bus boycott called *Stride Toward Freedom*. In September 1958 he was in a New York City bookstore autographing copies of the book when a black woman walked up to him and asked, "Is this Martin Luther King?" Then she stabbed him in the chest with a letter opener. King sat there, motionless. The doctors of Harlem Hospital later said that the seven-inch blade was touching the main artery leading from the heart. If King had not sat so calmly, he would have died. The surgeons knew he would always be marked by the scar and decided that since he was a minister, it should be cross-shaped.

The woman who stabbed King was taken to a mental hospital and diagnosed as insane.

Why did the Kings visit India?

In 1959 the Kings took a trip to India, even though Martin was supposed to be resting after the stabbing. For most people a tour of India wouldn't be restful, but it was more quiet than King's usual schedule. The Kings went to meet with the country's prime minister, Pandit Jawaharlal Nehru.

King also wanted to learn more about Gandhi's work. In India the lowest caste of people (called "untouchables" at the time) had been discriminated against in every way—until the government created and enforced laws against discrimination. Gandhi had led the way in this: He would often take an untouchable by the hand and lead him or her into the temples that had once been forbidden. Also, India was enforcing what we would now call an "affirmative action" program. If an untouchable and another person were equally qualified for admission to a university, the untouchable had to be admitted. Although some people wondered if this was not a kind of discrimination, the prime minister said it was fair. After centuries of enduring injustice, the untouchables deserved a break.

Then King returned to Alabama, which still had not integrated a single school. He believed more than ever in the need for nonviolent protest and in its power.

King had also seen the poverty in India, where millions of people lived on the streets, searching in garbage cans for food. Even when King was focused on voting rights and desegregation in America, he worried about the problems of poor people everywhere.

WHAT DOES IT MEAN?

India has a rigid social structure made up of four different classes, or **castes**. Once someone is born into a certain caste, it's impossible to move to another. The untouchables (called "dalits" today) are considered outside and below these four castes.

Why did the Kings move back to Atlanta?

King was seldom in Montgomery. When he was there, he was distracted. He once apologized for giving the same sermon three times, because he was too busy to write new ones. In Atlanta he would share the pulpit with his father (who was overjoyed to have him back) and his brother, A.D. He would have more time to organize the SCLC, which had its headquarters in Atlanta. King was tired and sometimes discouraged: The various black groups in Montgomery, which had been able to work together for the boycott, were not getting along anymore. Many people were mad that King had gotten most of the credit for the bus boycott.

King felt he must go forward. "I can't stop now," he told his Dexter congregation. "History has thrust something upon me which I cannot turn away from." He left Montgomery at the end of January 1960.

When is sitting down a hard, dangerous job?

Soon after King arrived in Atlanta, the executive director of the SCLC, Ella Baker, received an important phone call. It was from the Reverend Fred Shuttlesworth, who led the Birmingham branch of the SCLC. Shuttlesworth said she should tell King that "sit-ins might shake up the world."

On February 1, 1960, four black college students in Greensboro, North Carolina, asked to be served at a "white only" lunch counter in a Woolworth's department store. When they were refused service, they sat there until the store closed. For the next several days, dozens of students took turns sitting at the counter. No one would sell them even a cup of coffee. By the end of the week, a sign on the door said the store was closed "in the interest of public safety."

Meanwhile, college students in Nashville, Tennessee, had already been preparing for sit-ins. A divinity student, James Lawson, had spent three years in India learning about Gandhi's methods of nonviolent resistance. King had met Lawson in 1957, and he had urged Lawson to come south and become involved in the Civil Rights movement. Lawson organized workshops that attracted Diane Nash, a student from Chicago, and John Lewis, a student from another theological seminary in Nashville. They became leaders of the Nashville Student Movement. They were part of a generation of black students who had been inspired by what had happened in Montgomery.

Lawson taught the students to sit quietly and politely no matter what anyone said or did. They learned to protect their heads when attacked. The students who sat in at local lunch counters needed this training. Whites cursed them, threw pepper in their eyes, and ground burning cigarettes into their skin. The students sat still. Some prayed. When the police came, they arrested only the black students "for disturbing the peace."

Sit-ins were bad for business. Nashville store owners wanted their customers back. The arrests were bad publicity, because they showed that the South was not a place of "liberty and justice for all." (One governor was so annoyed by the TV coverage of the sit-ins that he claimed CBS was running them in order to have an exciting news story!)

The Nashville sit-ins showed what nonviolent protest could accomplish. The students got businesses to desegregate the lunch counters without help from the Supreme Court.

❝ The first sit-in we had was really funny. The waitresses were so nervous. They must have dropped $2,000 worth of dishes that day. . . . It was almost like a cartoon . . . we were sitting there trying not to laugh [but] at the same time were scared to death. **❞**

—**Diane Nash**, remembering her first sit-in, quoted in *Eyes on the Prize*, the 1987 documentary

What was "snick"?

John Lewis (left) prays with two other students in a demonstration.

King loved the sit-ins, recognizing them as a creative form of peaceful protest. On April 15, 1960, the Student Nonviolent Coordinating Committee (SNCC, pronounced "snick") was formed. Both King and Ella Baker had urged the students to form a national group. King hoped that the students would be part of the SCLC. Instead—with Baker's approval—they chose to form a separate group.

SNCC held sit-ins, wade-ins (at segregated pools), lie-ins (at segregated motels), and kneel-ins (at segregated churches).

Civil Rights Organizations: Which Group Is Which?

NAACP: The National Association for the Advancement of Colored People was founded on February 12, 1909 (Abraham Lincoln's birthday), to protect the rights—and lives—of black people. Most NAACP campaigns worked through government legislation or the courts rather than through boycotts or public protests. The NAACP has more than two thousand branches across the country today.

CORE: Started in 1942 by James Farmer, the Congress of Racial Equality seeks equal rights for black Americans. CORE organized sit-ins to protest segregation in restaurants and on buses and trains. It also organized voter registrations. Today the group's headquarters is in New York City.

WPC: The Women's Political Council was an organization of mostly middle-class, educated black women in Montgomery, Alabama. Formed in 1946 by Mary Fair Burks, the WPC wrote letters to the mayor, threatening a boycott if the buses were not desegregated.

MIA: The Montgomery Improvement Association was created in 1955 to organize the Montgomery Bus Boycott, and elected King as its president. It was unusual in its effort to be an organization of *all* black people in Montgomery. The MIA organized voter registration drives and worked for the integration of schools after the boycott.

SCLC: In 1957 King and some of his associates organized the Southern Christian Leadership Conference. It was an outgrowth of the success of the Montgomery Bus Boycott and the realization that ministers and churches were the most effective leaders of black protest. After King's death, Abernathy became the group's leader. Martin Luther King III served as president from 1997 to 2004.

SNCC: The Student Nonviolent Coordinating Committee was founded in 1960 by black college students who had been involved in the sit-in movement. They believed that their strength lay in their ability to work as a group without a single leader like King. The group later changed its name to the Student *National* Coordinating Committee, which showed that they no longer supported nonviolence and would fight back if attacked.

❝ Unless we can create the climate, the law can never bring victory. . . . All Africa will be free before the American Negro attains first-class citizenship. **❞**
—**James Lawson,** addressing the newly formed SNCC, 1960

Why didn't King join sit-ins in Atlanta at first?

King's father and his peers were the black leaders in Atlanta. "I grew up with these people," King told a friend. "They'll eat me alive if I make a mistake."

King promised the city's black leaders that he would not challenge their leadership of the Atlanta community. And this meant no sit-ins, because the men of his father's generation agreed with the NAACP: They believed Civil Rights should be won by lawyers in the courts, not by a bunch of college students "causing trouble."

Besides, one of the sit-ins in Atlanta was going to be at Rich's department store, where black families were allowed to have credit cards just like whites. Credit cards were far less common in 1960 than they are today, and Atlanta blacks were proud of their Rich's credit cards—even if they were still banned from eating at the store's restaurant, the Magnolia Room.

But by October 1960, the sit-in movement in Atlanta needed a boost, and the students told King he was it. So King agreed to sit-in with them at the Magnolia Room and to be arrested with them. He was. He spent the next few days in jail, discussing nonviolence and losing checker games to the local student leader.

But when the students were released, King was not.

Why did the sit-in arrest get King into big trouble?

Earlier that year, King had been
stopped by the police simply
because he and his wife were in
the car with a white woman, a
friend they'd had dinner
with. Then the policeman
discovered that King's
driver's license had
expired, and so he put
King on probation. After
the sit-in arrest, a Georgia
state judge used this earlier
"crime" against him, ruling
that King had broken his
probation. He sentenced
King to four months of hard
labor at the state prison.
Coretta Scott King cried in the
courtroom—one of the few times
anyone saw her lose control in public.

In the middle of the night, the jailer took King from
his cell and put handcuffs and leg irons on him. He
was driven for hours through the night. King felt
terrified and thought for sure that he would be
killed, which happened often to black prisoners.
Even after he was delivered to the state prison, he
knew he was not safe. He was cold and frightened,
and he hated being alone. Being alone gave him too
much time to worry. Later he would try to make sure
that Abernathy was always with him in jail.

How did King's imprisonment affect the outcome of the 1960 presidential election?

Unable to get news of her husband, Coretta Scott King called Harris Wofford, a friend who worked for Senator John F. Kennedy's election campaign. He had written a book on Gandhian nonviolence and had been introduced to the Kings a few years earlier by Bayard Rustin.

Democrat John F. Kennedy was running for president against Republican candidate Vice President Richard Nixon. Neither wanted to get involved with King's arrest, because they were afraid of losing the white southern vote, but Wofford persuaded Kennedy to call Coretta and say he was concerned. John F. Kennedy's younger brother and campaign manager, attorney Robert Kennedy, went further and yelled at the judge. He said it was illegal to sentence someone without bail for a misdemeanor, or minor crime. The judge decided that he could let King out on probation after all.

Nixon, who had met the Kings three years earlier in Ghana, thought that what the judge had done was wrong, too. But he didn't call anyone and had "no comment" when reporters asked him about King's imprisonment.

Without telling the Kennedys, election workers printed millions of leaflets titled "'No Comment' Nixon Versus a Candidate with a Heart, Senator Kennedy." King's father, who had always been a Republican and had said he would never vote for a Catholic, said, "I have all my votes and I've got a suitcase, and I'm going to take them . . . [and] dump them in [Kennedy's] lap."

Out of the blacks who could vote, more voted for a Democrat than ever before. Kennedy won the election. Republican President Eisenhower complained that Kennedy won because of his call to Coretta Scott King.

What was it like to be part of the King family?

Yoki and Marty were very young when their father went to jail for the first time. Marty, age three, asked if Daddy had gone to jail in an airplane. (He was used to his father flying everywhere.) But Yoki was five and old enough to ask why her daddy was in jail. She was told that he went to jail to help people.

Martin and Coretta with Marty and Yoki

Yoki was starting to learn about segregation. The next year she wanted to go to an amusement park called Funtown because the TV ads said all children should come. After she begged to go, her parents told her the truth: Only white children could go to Funtown. A few years later, when Funtown was desegregated, the Kings finally went. Yoki knew that her father had helped make that visit possible.

Being Martin Luther King's child was hard. When Yoki was seven, she complained to her classmates that she just wanted to be treated like a normal kid. Marty once pretended that he didn't know his father's name. He was afraid he would get beat up by white kids who didn't like what his father was doing. But when he started third grade, a white boy said to him, "Your father's that famous nigger." Marty responded firmly, "The word is 'Negro.'"

Coretta Scott King tried to make the children's lives as normal as possible while Martin was away from home. He missed his children's birthdays, yet they still knew that he loved them. He loved to play games with them when he was home. He'd let them climb on top of the refrigerator and jump into his arms. Coretta wished they wouldn't do that. And when they'd play basketball in the house on a rainy day, she'd say, "Martin, please don't play ball in the house," as though he were a child. And, like a child, he'd say there was no place else to play.

LIVING IN HIS SHADOW

Being King's brother was hard too. A.D. had never had his brother's ability to just walk away from an argument with their father. Now that his famous brother was back, he felt as if he was living in his shadow. In 1961, he moved to Birmingham to be a minister there.

Coretta would always worry about her husband's safety, but also she got angry when he was away all the time. He wouldn't let her travel with him very often or risk getting arrested, which she wanted to do. He said she had to be home to take care of the children. And in January 1961, there was another child to take care of—a son, Dexter, named after the Kings' old church in Montgomery.

Since King was so famous, was he rich?

A lot of people thought King must be rich, but then they'd see his old car and think differently. And his family lived in a small rented house in a poor part of the city, not the wealthier section where his parents lived. In fact, he didn't want money, and he donated much of the money he earned instead of keeping it for himself.

Yet King still liked expensive suits, as he had as a teenager. He didn't really think he should want silk suits when so many people were poor, but he liked them anyway. When he was in jail for protests, he would try to have someone bring him silk pajamas.

What were the freedom rides?

In 1960 the courts had banned segregated waiting rooms, bathrooms, and restaurants in interstate bus and train stations. But southern states ignored the court's ruling. King had spoken to President Kennedy about this, but with little success. He was made aware of the problem but was not willing to address it with legislation. However, James Farmer from CORE planned to challenge the government to enforce its own rules. Trained volunteers, both black and white, would ride buses through the South, stopping at stations and testing if the waiting rooms were integrated.

On May 4, 1961, two buses of freedom riders left from Washington, D.C. The first few days were peaceful. Blacks were ordered out of some white-only waiting rooms, but they were not harmed. Then, on May 14, a mob in Anniston, Alabama, shot out the tires of one bus and threw a bomb into the window. Many riders were attacked as they escaped the burning bus.

The other bus arrived in Birmingham. Reporters who had been waiting there recorded how the riders were beaten by a mob armed with chains and baseball bats. The police had told the Ku Klux Klan that they could have fifteen minutes before the cops would interfere. The FBI had known this and done nothing.

Diane Nash of SNCC volunteered members of the Nashville Student Movement to join the riders. She said if they let violence stop them, then "the movement was dead."

With a promise of state police protection from Governor John Patterson, the rides continued through Alabama, surrounded by police cars on the road and planes flying overhead. But before the bus entered the Montgomery station, the state police cars left and the local police, promised to replace them, never came. A mob poured in from all directions, beating at least three riders unconscious.

AMERICAN VOICES

❝ We planned the freedom rides with the specific intention of creating a crisis. . . . We figured that the government would have to respond if we created a situation that was headline news all over the world. ❞

—James Farmer

How did King respond to the freedom rides?

King flew to Montgomery to hold a mass meeting at the First Baptist Church. Federal marshals surrounded the church, but they could not control the huge mob that gathered that night. Fearing that the mob would firebomb the building, King called Robert Kennedy, now U.S. attorney general. He also calmed the people inside. Kennedy threatened Alabama governor John Patterson that he would send in federal troops. By dawn, the state police and National Guard were escorting people out of the church and to safety.

King walked the freedom riders to their bus but said he could not go with them to their next stop in Mississippi. He was still on probation, and another arrest would have meant serious jail time. It was a decision that widened the gap between King and SNCC. The riders were furious with King. The director of the FBI, J. Edgar Hoover, had told the Kennedys that King was a national danger, but the students found him too conservative.

As soon as the freedom riders integrated the waiting rooms of the Jackson, Mississippi, bus station, they were marched to jail. Refusing bail, they went to state prisons and endured beatings. When the guards threatened to take away their mattresses if they wouldn't stop singing freedom songs, they slept on cold metal bed frames.

On November 1, 1961, at Robert Kennedy's insistence, the Interstate Commerce Commission banned segregation of waiting rooms, bathrooms, and eating places at interstate bus and train stations.

Did protests always work?

In November 1961 two of the freedom riders decided to test the Interstate Commerce Commission's recent ruling in Albany, a small city in Georgia. Along with some other SNCC members, they went to a white-only waiting room at a bus station and the police told them to get out. They did. A few people getting arrested wouldn't do any good; they just wanted people to know that the new laws hadn't changed anything. Waiting rooms were still white only.

Later protesters were arrested at the bus station, and gradually protests against all segregation in Albany began to build. But no matter how many people were arrested or how many demonstrations were held, no one seemed to notice.

Police Chief Laurie Pritchett had done his homework. He had studied a map and worked out where he could send prisoners. That way protesters couldn't pack the jails until he ran out of places to put them. Pritchett had read about the nonviolence movement. He realized that if he kept all the arrests peaceful, the press wouldn't report it. (He also arrested the students for disorderly conduct and other minor crimes not related to segregation, so that no one would dispute the arrests.)

Pritchett was right. Reporters congratulated Pritchett for keeping order. No one mentioned that students were still being removed from a waiting room that the law said was integrated.

William Anderson, head of the Albany movement, asked King to come to Georgia. On December 15 King and Abernathy arrived, and King led a march the next day. He, Abernathy, and two hundred others were arrested. When King was tried and found guilty, he said he would not pay the fine; he would go to jail instead, in order to put pressure on the city. The mayor had someone pay King's and Abernathy's fines and—against their will—they were released.

The protesters battled on for many months. At last the city got a ruling from a federal judge forbidding any more demonstrations; King decided, after much

King and Abernathy together in prison

thought, to honor it. After all, a presidential order had desegregated the military several years before. A Supreme Court decision had said school segregation was unconstitutional. King was counting on further help from the federal government against state and city laws. But King's willingness to follow the federal order angered SNCC.

Although SNCC continued their protests, the Albany movement failed. The protests hadn't been planned well. People had demonstrated against the city, not against the businesses. Their demands hadn't been clear enough. And Laurie Pritchett had kept the press on his side.

AMERICAN VOICES

66 I've been thrown out of lots of places in my day, but never before have I been thrown out of a jail. 99
—Reverend Ralph Abernathy

What hadn't happened to King in six years?

He had not led a Civil Rights victory.

FREEDOM SONGS

Music and singing had always been important in black churches and life. African Americans have a history of protest music. They sang about pain and about hope for freedom and justice. Slaves had sung Christian spirituals while they worked in the fields. Owners didn't always notice that some of these songs were about freedom or rebellion. During the Montgomery bus boycott, singing at mass meetings had helped people stay peaceful and gave them strength. Music brought comfort and drew people together.

Some of the Civil Rights songs, such as "We Shall Overcome," were based on union songs. Workers would sing these tunes when they banded together to protest for their rights. Religious songs were also adapted. A song of just one word—"Amen"—became another one-word tune called "Freedom."

People in photos of peaceful protests don't usually look afraid, but they sometimes admitted that they were scared inside. Singing helped to calm them. Songs have power—national anthems, cheers, the tunes soldiers sing when marching out to battle. If people sing together, they feel stronger.

Songs also gave the protesters an advantage over the police and the hate-filled mobs. People armed with guns or clubs seemed to find it disconcerting to hit people whose only weapon was a song.

CHAPTER 5

Bombingham

Funeral for a girl killed in a Birmingham church bombing

Why was Birmingham, Alabama, nicknamed "Bombingham"?

Bombings were common in Birmingham; between 1947 and 1963, fifty black homes were blasted. No one was ever punished at the time. It was a city of killings and cross burnings. King had been punched there as he spoke at a 1962 SCLC meeting. (True to his nonviolent principles, he did not defend himself.) The most violent beatings of the freedom riders had taken place in Birmingham. Rather than integrate its parks, playgrounds, pools, and golf courses, as the federal court had said it must, the city closed them.

Eugene "Bull" Connor, the commissioner of public safety, enforced the violence and segregation. When students boycotted stores and business owners integrated lunch counters and restrooms, Connor forced them to put their white-only signs back up. When George Wallace was elected governor of Alabama, the crowd cheered his inauguration speech in January 1963 as he shouted, "Segregation now! Segregation tomorrow! Segregation forever!"

King, Abernathy, and Shuttlesworth planned Birmingham as the next focus for the movement. The SCLC's Wyatt T. Walker said later, "We knew that as Birmingham went, so would go the South. And we felt that if we could crack that city, then we could crack any city."

What was "Project C"?

C stood for "confrontation."

The SCLC planned to create a situation that would build, day by day. Starting on April 3, 1963, they would boycott white businesses. These stores needed blacks to buy from them, since 40 percent of

FRED SHUTTLESWORTH: FIERCE DEFENDER OF CIVIL RIGHTS

In 1956 Reverend Fred Shuttlesworth had organized a bus boycott in Birmingham modeled on the one in Montgomery. He was almost killed when segregationists blew up his house but said he would not "run away." He did not run after his church was bombed or, later, when he and his wife were attacked for trying to enroll their children in a white school. King once called him "the most courageous Civil Rights fighter in the South." Shuttlesworth worked steadily with SCLC's Birmingham branch to desegregate public places.

the people in the city were black. The protesters would fill the jails until Connor couldn't arrest any more people because he would have nowhere to put them. They knew Connor would lose his temper and show the world the violence that blacks in Birmingham lived with all the time. The press would cover it, and then the federal government would have to act.

AMERICAN VOICES

66 The movement was really about getting publicity for injustice. . . . As long as it stayed below the surface, no one was concerned about it. You had to bring it into the open. 99

—Andrew Young

What did black citizens of Birmingham think of King's arrival in town?

Some black business owners worried. Successful owners had a lot to lose. They had money and the respect of the black community. King believed that kind of respectability cost too much. It ignored what was happening to the rest of the blacks.

Other people asked why this young guy was "stepping out," or behaving in a way that black people weren't supposed to. It was like "stepping out of line"—and it could get you killed. Some people would say that King was stirring up whites, and others would say that they needed to be stirred up. Church attendance picked up, since people wanted to hear the news, and that was the best place to get it.

No one knew what would happen.

When King first spoke in Birmingham, people came out two or three hours early to get seats in the church. Those who came later stood outside and listened to him on loudspeakers. People came who never thought they'd march, and then they did. King warned them how dangerous it would be to end segregation in Birmingham. He said, "Don't ever be afraid to die. . . . You must say somehow, 'I don't have much money. I don't have much education. I may not be able to read and write; but I do have the capacity to die.'"

"He took all the fear out of you," said nineteen-year-old Geneva Jones.

How did Martin Luther King celebrate Easter weekend in 1963?

People marched the week before Easter, and Connor arrested them. But the jails weren't full, and they were running out of "jail volunteers," or people who were willing to be arrested. The newspapers criticized King, saying that it was the Civil Rights workers causing the problems, not the segregationists. Also, the SCLC ministers were supposed to be back in their home churches, preaching on Easter Sunday.

On the morning of Friday, April 12, King and about twenty-four other people involved in the protests—including his father and brother—met at King's headquarters in Birmingham's Gaston Motel. Daddy King wanted his son back home. Other people said that King should lead a protest and be arrested. Then others would volunteer. Still others pointed out that the SCLC was broke, and they needed King to go on a fund-raising tour. Although they planned to fill the jails, they had to be able to bail people out and pay fines eventually: People had jobs to go to and families to feed. No one wanted the Birmingham protests to end as the Albany ones had, with nothing accomplished.

King's father, brother, and his SCLC staff shouted and argued about what to do next. King listened quietly. Then he went into another room and prayed. When he came out, he was wearing blue jeans. He always wore jeans when he went to jail, so everyone knew what he had decided.

That day King and Abernathy were arrested leading a march to City Hall. King had been arrested before, but this was the first time he had *tried* to be arrested.

❝ Well, you didn't get this nonviolence from me. You must have got it from your mama. ❞
    —**Reverend Martin Luther King Senior,** 1963

Why did King need so much paper in jail?

The police threw King in solitary confinement, in a cell without a mattress or pillow. Not until Coretta Scott King called the White House did anyone know if he was even alive. John and Robert Kennedy both called Birmingham government officials. King said later that he had wondered why the guards suddenly started to treat him better.

While King was in jail, eight white clergymen published a letter in the *Birmingham News*. They said the Birmingham protest was "unwise and untimely," and the SCLC should not break laws and stir up "hatred and violence." King wrote them an answer. He began writing on the edges of newspapers and even on toilet paper. Through his prison bars he would pass what he'd written to a friend and say, "I need more paper."

Quoting from the Old and New Testaments of the Bible, King said he believed that people had a responsibility to break unjust laws, though they must do it peacefully and accept the punishment for breaking them. "Injustice anywhere is a threat to justice everywhere," he wrote. He also wrote that black people had waited 340 years, since the first slaves were brought to America, for their rights. They had lived in fear, in danger, always waiting, all that time. The white clergymen had not lived with that fear, he wrote, or else they would not say "wait."

None of the clergymen responded to King's letter.

When were the jails of Birmingham packed with children?

Regretfully, King's imprisonment did not produce more volunteers. So James Bevel, one of King's close advisers, suggested that they have children demonstrate. A lot of people, including King, thought this was a terrible idea. Suppose a child was killed? But Bevel said it would work. If the police jailed children, the city would look terrible—and children didn't have to worry about losing their jobs.

Thousands of teenagers and children as young as six years old were trained in nonviolent protest techniques. They dressed neatly and marched from the Sixteenth Street Baptist Church toward the downtown shopping area of Birmingham singing, "We shall overcome some day." The police arrested more than nine hundred the first day, and more kept coming. By the next day, Bull Connor had police dogs ready—and fire hoses. These weren't garden hoses; they blasted water with so much force it knocked people off their feet, tore their clothes off, and pushed them through the air into walls or cars.

The next day more children came. Connor kept the dogs and hoses coming too. And news reporters kept coming. All over the world, people watched the city's firemen blast children with water cannons, while Connor yelled, "Look at those niggers run!" They saw that Birmingham would attack little kids to keep black people from eating at a lunch counter. "It makes me sick," said President Kennedy.

❝ We're supposed to fight fires, not people. ❞

—An angry Birmingham fireman, 1963, as later told to a *Life* magazine photographer

How did the Birmingham protests end?

Business owners couldn't afford to lose money. And besides, no one could afford the trouble caused by 170 news reporters broadcasting such terrible things about their city.

The protesters and business community leaders reached an agreement. Store fitting rooms and lunch counters would be desegregated immediately, and water fountains would be next. Businesses would hire black workers.

Then the riots broke out.

Bull Connor and the Ku Klux Klan said that the merchants had no right to make deals with protesters. A. D. King's house was bombed; so was the Gaston Motel. The local police and state troopers were called in. Seven stores burned and thirty-five blacks were injured. President Kennedy called in the federal troops, but stationed them thirty miles outside Birmingham. The troops were a threat: He would send them in if state and local authorities could not restore order. He also spoke on national television in favor of the settlement that had been reached and in favor of new Civil Rights laws.

King said Birmingham was the biggest victory of the Civil Rights movement. Without help from the courts, ordinary people protested, risked their lives, went to jail—and caused the city to change its laws.

AMERICAN VOICES

❝ We are confronted primarily with a moral issue. It is as old as the Scriptures and as clear as the American Constitution. If an American, because his skin is dark, cannot eat lunch in a restaurant open to the public, if he cannot send his children to the best public schools available . . . then who among us would be content to have the color of his skin changed? Who among us would then be content with counsels of patience and delay? . . .

"I am therefore asking the Congress to enact legislation giving all Americans the right to be served in facilities which are open to the public—hotels, restaurants, theaters, retail stores, and similar establishments. This seems to me an elementary right. ❞

—**President John Kennedy**, June 11, 1963, as he presented Congress with a new Civil Rights bill

What was the "March on Washington"?

A. Philip Randolph, who organized the march with Bayard Rustin, called it "The March on Washington for Jobs and Freedom." The march, which was planned to end with a rally on the mall, would demand a two-dollar-an-hour minimum wage, the desegregation of schools, and federal action to end racial discrimination in employment. It would be the biggest Civil Rights demonstration ever and would show Congress how much support there was for President Kennedy's Civil Rights bill.

On August 27, 1963, volunteers at New York City's Riverside Church

> **WHAT DOES IT MEAN?**
>
> A **bill** is a proposed law. It doesn't become an actual law until it is passed by the two chambers of Congress and signed by the president.

made eighty thousand cheese sandwiches for people going to the march. But that was nothing compared to what the organizers had to do. They thought about a hundred thousand people might come. Would there be enough water for everyone? Where would a hundred thousand people go to the toilet?

At first President Kennedy and Congress thought the march was a terrible idea. They weren't worrying about drinking water or toilets; they were worried about riots. But when it was clear that the march would go on, Kennedy said he supported it. He believed in what the march stood for. Hospitals in Washington, D.C., prepared for injuries caused by rioting.

Early in the morning of August 28, Courtland Cox of SNCC and Bayard Rustin stood on the empty mall.

"Suppose no one comes?" asked Rustin. Almost at that very moment a bus arrived from the Virginia NAACP. They explained that people weren't there yet because every road to Washington had a traffic jam. *Everyone* was coming to the march. One man came from Chicago—almost eight hundred miles away—on roller skates.

More than 250,000 people marched in Washington that day.

WHAT DO THEY SELL IN THE NATIONAL MALL?

Before "mall" meant an indoor place to shop, it meant an open place to walk. The National Mall in Washington is a two-and-one-half-mile park that stretches from the U.S. Capitol to the Potomac River and includes the Washington Monument, the Reflecting Pool, and the Lincoln Memorial.

Was the march a success?

Celebrities such as Joan Baez, Sammy Davis Jr., and Marian Anderson performed. Then Randolph introduced King to the crowd as the "moral leader of the nation."

King stood in front of the Lincoln Memorial and asked what had become of that promise of freedom—the promise that blacks, too, had the rights of "life, liberty, and the pursuit of happiness"? The promise had not been honored, said King. Now it must be. And in spite of the problems the Civil Rights movement had faced, King still had his dream. He wanted the nation to live up to the words in the Declaration of Independence: "All men are created equal."

"I have a dream," said King, "that my four little children will one day live in a nation where they will not be judged by the color of their skin but by the content of their character." He said that it was not until black people were free that all people would be free, and could "sing in the words of the old spiritual, 'Free at last! Free at last! Thank God Almighty, we're free at last!'"

The march created tremendous hope. Many people of different races, from all over the country, were united for justice that day. The event was carried live on all three major TV networks. It was the first time millions of Americans had heard King speak. That speech confirmed his status as the voice of the Civil Rights movement.

John Lewis, from SNCC, also spoke at the march. He wanted to say that Kennedy's Civil Rights bill didn't do enough and that black people should march through the South and "burn Jim Crow to the ground, nonviolently." Only Randolph could persuade Lewis to rewrite his speech—which he did, angrily, on a portable typewriter behind the statue of Lincoln.

Rosa Parks later wrote that no women were allowed to speak, even though Parks, Daisy Bates, Diane Nash, Ella Baker, and many others who had been crucial to the movement were present. The women weren't even allowed to march with the men, said Coretta Scott King. She also wanted to go with her husband when he and the march's leaders met with the president afterward, but none of the women was invited.

How did the segregationists respond to the march?

On September 15, 1963, some white men threw dynamite through an open window of Birmingham's Sixteenth Street Baptist Church just as Sunday school began. Four girls—one aged eleven and three aged fourteen—died. More than twenty other people

were pulled from the wreckage. Although African American churches had always been the targets of bombings, this was the first time segregationists had bombed a church when they knew it would be full. Nothing could have hurt or angered the black community more than an attack on their children, in their church—the one place they had always been safe.

Did King still believe in the nonviolent movement after this church bombing?

The nonviolent Civil Rights movement barely survived the attack on the Sixteenth Street Baptist Church. Others were killed, and blacks were arming themselves to fight back. King told the press that the president should send the army to take over the city and keep order. The president didn't. It was the end of the nonviolent movement, said someone who spoke at the funeral of three of the girls. King disagreed. He said that only the "ammunition of love" could fight hate and save the soul of America. But friends watching him speak thought he looked as if he might fall over. He said he had the "weight of the world" on him.

Two months after the church bombing, President Kennedy was assassinated. King and his family mourned the president's death. Yoki, who had just turned eight, was in despair: She thought it was unjust that a good man had died. "We're never going to get our freedom now," she wailed.

Thirty-four-year-old King saw again the danger he was in. "I don't think I'm going to reach forty," he told his wife.

Was Martin Luther King excited about being named *Time* magazine's "Man of the Year"?

At the end of 1963, King learned that he would be the first African American to be "man of the year." It was a great honor—one of many he would win that year—but he was too tired to enjoy it. It had been a long year of victories and deaths, of giving more than 350 speeches and traveling 275,000 miles. Besides, *Time*'s article about him said he had no sense of humor, which didn't please him any.

MARTY GOES TO FLORIDA

In June 1964 King flew to St. Augustine, Florida, for a protest march. Friends and coworkers were surprised to see seven-year-old Marty there with his father. King said he had so little time with his children and it was so impossible to protect them from danger that he had decided to bring his elder son with him. Marty didn't know what was going on. As an adult he said that at the time, he didn't understand they were marching for a cause. He just thought marches were something his family did.

What was the Civil Rights Act of 1964?

Martin Luther King was in the White House on July 2 when President Lyndon B. Johnson (who had been Kennedy's vice president) signed the Civil Rights bill, making it into law. (He used seventy-two pens so that they could be souvenirs!)

Congress had finally voted yes on Kennedy's Civil Rights bill. Segregation in all public places became illegal. Denying someone a job because of his or her skin color became illegal.

President Johnson suggested to King and the other black leaders that, with this new law, demonstrations would no longer be necessary. King knew this wasn't true. The new law did not yet address one important issue: the need for the federal government to make sure that blacks could register to vote. Still, it was the best Civil Rights law that had been passed, because it made segregation illegal under the laws of the land.

Where was Martin Luther King when he found out he had won the Nobel Peace Prize?

In Atlanta's St. Joseph's Infirmary. He wasn't sick, but he was so exhausted that he had gone into the hospital for tests. When his wife called to

King receives the Nobel Peace Prize in 1964.

tell him about the prize, he thought he was dreaming. The Nobel Peace Prize is awarded each year "for the most effective work in the interests of international peace." At age thirty-five, King was the youngest person ever to win the prize.

On December 10, 1964, King received his prize in Oslo, Norway. He hated his formal striped pants, gray tailcoat, and ascot he couldn't tie; he said he'd never wear anything like them again. The head of the prize committee said King was "the first person in the Western world to have shown us that struggle can be waged without violence."

King often worried if he was doing the right thing. There were always people telling him he was wrong: SNCC kept telling him he was too conservative and careful, and the NAACP kept telling him to use court cases and the law instead of protests. Now he was being told that his work was so important to the whole world that he deserved this prize.

King was given a check for about fifty-four thousand dollars. Coretta wanted some of the money for their children's college fund, but King had never kept more than a few thousand dollars of the hundreds of thousands he earned making speeches. And Abernathy thought he should have shared in the prize, as he had been at King's side for so much of the time since Montgomery. But King gave the money to various Civil Rights organizations instead.

Who called King "the most notorious liar in the country"?

The director of the FBI, J. Edgar Hoover did, soon after hearing that King would receive the Nobel Peace Prize. Hoover did not say what King was lying about, but hinted that he had done terrible things.

Hoover had hated King for years. He didn't like blacks and especially didn't like King, who fought for social change. He had gotten permission from Robert Kennedy to wiretap King's phone by saying that King associated with communists and was a national danger. (Many Americans in the 1950s and early 1960s feared communism, which was associated with the Soviet Union and the fight for world power.) It was true that King's friend Stanley

Levison had given money to the communist party many years earlier, but King was not a communist.

Once Hoover had wiretaps of King's life, he had new ammunition. King told dirty jokes. King had sex with women who weren't his wife. So had President Kennedy—and Hoover could prove it—which is why no one could get rid of Hoover. He had been the director of the FBI since its formation in 1924 and knew everyone's secrets.

What secrets arrived in a box?

Coretta Scott King opened a box sent by the FBI to her husband before he went to Norway. It contained a reel of recording tape and a letter that said King was "filthy" and "evil." "There is but one way out for you. You better take it." The letter may have meant for King to kill himself rather than accept the Nobel Prize. Instead he played the tape, made up of FBI wiretaps, to his closest coworkers. Of course King couldn't tell everyone about the FBI or about his girlfriends, but the sermons he preached at that time may have shown what he was feeling about his behavior. He said he had never claimed to be a great role model, but he tried to be the best he could and to redeem himself and America through the movement. He said that we all had a higher self and a lower self, and that we needed to struggle against that lower self. King worried about his wife being hurt and angry, and he felt guilty because he didn't think he had behaved well either.

Although he exhausted himself with worry about Hoover, King kept traveling and speaking.

CHAPTER 6

Bloody Sunday

Protesters in front of the state capitol in Montgomery

Why did King and the Civil Rights movement go to Selma, Alabama?

Selma was in Dallas County, where only three hundred of the twenty-eight thousand black citizens could vote. (In two other Alabama counties, *no* blacks could vote.) In Selma the registrar's office was open only two days a month. The registrars came in late, took long lunches, and left early.

The Civil Rights workers wanted the federal government to send in its own people to register voters. "Wait," said President Johnson. He believed it was too soon after the 1964 Civil Rights Act for him to ask Congress to pass a voting act. But the Fifteenth Amendment to the Constitution had given blacks the right to vote back in 1870. They had waited too long already.

What happened when King went to Selma?

On January 2, 1965, King addressed seven hundred people in Selma's Brown Chapel. "We are demanding the ballot," said King. They were not just asking, but *demanding*.

Peaceful demonstrations and marches to the courthouse failed to provoke Sheriff Jim Clark into violence, so newspapers and television stations didn't report the story. Four hundred people would march to the courthouse on registration days, demanding to register to vote. The sheriff would tell everyone to line up in a back alley and wait to be called to register. They would wait all day without a single person even being given the tests.

On January 19 people waiting to register didn't move to the alley fast enough to suit Sheriff Clark. He grabbed one woman and started shoving her down the street with his billy club. The other protesters—and the national TV and newspaper reporters—saw it all. People pushed inside the courthouse and were arrested.

Then something important happened: The schoolteachers marched. In black communities the teachers were one of the most respected groups, but they had to worry about losing their jobs because the school boards that hired them were white. When the teachers marched—holding up toothbrushes, the sign that they were willing to go to jail—everyone marched. The undertakers marched. The hairstylists marched. And the schoolchildren marched.

On February 1 King was arrested. The police said that he didn't leave big enough gaps between each group of people marching to the courthouse. As in Birmingham, King's arrest was intended to encourage volunteers and to get the attention of reporters. While King was in jail, SNCC invited Malcolm X to town to speak. He was one of the new young black leaders who most disagreed with King's nonviolent campaigns. While saying positive things about King, he also spoke to the Selma crowd about the need for blacks to defend themselves. His speech was met with mixed responses. "I didn't

come to Selma to make [King's] job difficult," he later told Coretta Scott King. "I really did come thinking that I could make it easier. If white people realize what the alternative is, perhaps they would be more willing to listen to Dr. King."

Malcolm X

When Malcolm X was born, his name was Malcolm Little. In 1952 he said that he would no longer use that name. It was his "slave name," the name of the man who had once owned his family. His own family's name could never be known, and so he would call himself X, a letter which is sometimes used to mean "unknown."

As a young man, Malcolm X believed that blacks didn't need to be integrated into white culture. Instead they needed to have their own culture and economy and not depend on the "white devils" for anything. In 1964 he changed his views and said that blacks should work with Latinos and whites to create a better society for all.

Three weeks after he spoke in Selma, Malcolm X was assassinated in Harlem by members of the Black Muslim group he had separated from.

Why was a march planned from Selma to Montgomery?

King sent a letter from the Selma jail to the *New York Times*. He said, "There are more Negroes in jail with me than there are on the voting rolls."

Demonstrations spread to nearby counties. One nighttime march resulted in the first death of the Selma campaign. When the streetlights went out, police and local whites began attacking the marchers. Twenty-six-year-old Jimmie Lee Jackson saw his grandfather injured and took him and his mother into a café for safety. State troopers followed them and hit Mrs. Jackson. When Jimmie Lee

Jackson defended his mother, the police shot him. He died a few days later.

James Bevel, who had suggested filling the jails of Birmingham with children, left Jackson's funeral saying he wanted to march the fifty-four miles to Montgomery and tell Governor Wallace just how mad he was.

What was "Bloody Sunday"?

On Sunday, March 7, about six hundred people gathered at Brown Chapel and began their march to the capitol. The march organizers expected people to be arrested. Governor Wallace had told the state police that they could do whatever they wanted to stop the march.

King was home in Atlanta. In the past two months, he had led marches, held meetings, and traveled to New York, Michigan, and Washington, D.C., to talk with the president about a voting act. He was in poor health. King agreed that the march could go on while he was away, but joked that he didn't want *all* of them to get arrested.

Two by two, the marchers walked the six blocks to the Edmund Pettus Bridge, carrying bag lunches, backpacks, and bedrolls. They looked like people going on a picnic. The marchers crossed the bridge, but they couldn't see what was waiting on the other side. Then they saw state troopers wearing gas masks and carrying nightsticks, whips, and clubs wrapped in barbed wire. When the marchers were fifty feet away, the head trooper ordered them to stop. The demonstrators were standing motionless when he commanded, "Troopers, advance!" A triangular wedge of troopers smashed through the line of marchers, knocking people to the ground and trampling them. As the demonstrators began to run back toward safety, the troopers chased them, hitting them with nightsticks and whips. Police on horseback rode through the screaming crowd. White spectators cheered.

Suddenly there was a noise that sounded like a gunshot. Just before news reporters lost sight of the demonstration in a gray cloud of tear gas, they saw nightsticks rise and fall on the heads of fleeing marchers. Others saw the police use whips as the crying, half-blinded, vomiting crowd tried to return to Brown Chapel, pursued right to its door.

America watched this happen on their televisions. TV stations interrupted their regular programs to show what was happening in Selma, on the day that would be called "Bloody Sunday."

❝ IMPORTANT YOU TAKE IMMEDIATE ACTION IN
ALABAMA ONE MORE DAY OF SAVAGE TREATMENT
BY LEGALIZED HATCHET MEN COULD LEAD TO
OPEN WARFARE BY AROUSED NEGROES AMERICA
CANNOT AFFORD THIS IN 1965 **❞**
—Telegram from **Jackie Robinson** to President Johnson,
March 9, 1965

Why did Martin Luther King honor a federal ruling forbidding the next Selma to Montgomery march?

King was not the only one horrified by the brutal beatings. People watching it on TV cried or turned their faces away. One station had been showing a movie about Nazi Germany, and when the beatings were broadcast, viewers thought at first they were watching Nazi storm troopers at work. Thousands of people, black and white, traveled to Selma to march and to support black citizens' right to vote. King and the SCLC invited hundreds of clergy to march with them. The Civil Rights movement had changed a lot since the days of the Montgomery bus boycott when whites, including ministers, were afraid to show their support.

But a federal judge said that the march could not take place yet. He wanted to look into what had happened and to consider the protesters' request for protection. In the meantime President Johnson was trying to get the Voting Rights Act passed—the law that would give the protesters what they were asking for. King wanted this law to be passed so, as he had in Albany, he honored the federal judge's ruling.

He worked out a compromise: On March 9, two thousand protesters would march to the bridge, pray, and then turn back. This would be a demonstration of their feelings but, since they would not be leaving Selma, it would not go against the court order. But not everyone knew of this plan. SNCC and many of the people who had come to town for this march would not have agreed. So when King led people to the bridge and turned back, they were first confused, then angry. They thought King had chickened out.

That night a white minister from Boston, James Reeb, was clubbed to death leaving a Selma restaurant. His death was covered widely by the news, although Jimmie Lee Jackson's had not been.

❝❝ It is wrong—deadly wrong—to deny any of your fellow Americans the right to vote. . . . We have already waited one hundred years and more, and the time for waiting is gone.

"This time, on this issue, there must be no delay, no hesitation, and no compromise with our purpose. . . .

"What happened in Selma was an American tragedy. The blows that were received, the blood that was shed, the life of the good man that was lost, must strengthen the determination of each of us to bring full equality and equal justice to all of our people. This is not just the policy of your government or your president. It is in the heart and the purpose and the meaning of America itself. . . .

"Their cause must be our cause, too. Because it is not just Negroes, but it's really all of us who must overcome the crippling legacy of bigotry and injustice.

"And we shall overcome. 💬"

—**Lyndon B. Johnson**, addressing Congress and the American people, March 15, 1965

What was the final Selma to Montgomery march for?

On March 15 President Johnson addressed the American people, presenting the voting rights bill and asking Congress to pass it quickly. Tears rolled down King's face as Johnson spoke.

The last march was in support of the bill and a demand that it be made into law immediately. But the marchers still needed protection. After President Johnson spoke, the Montgomery County sheriff's deputies had attacked SNCC protesters with clubs and whips. Governor Wallace said he wouldn't pay for police protection for a bunch of "communist-trained anarchists." So President Johnson federalized the Alabama National Guard. About four thousand members of the Alabama guard, the army, and the FBI would guard the march.

Around four thousand others would start the march, but most would have to turn back after seven miles. The judge had said that once the road narrowed from four lanes to two, there would be too many people blocking the road. So three hundred people were chosen to march the whole way. The rest of the people could meet the marchers for the last miles and then gather at the state capitol in Montgomery.

The march took five days. Martin Luther King and his wife marched together for much of it. The group was made of blacks and whites, Christians and Jews, housewives, college students, and children. Segregationists along the route held signs or painted threats on cars, such as: "Yankee trash go home" or "Open Season on Niggers!—Cheap Ammo Here." Marchers ignored them; instead, they added new verses to "We Shall Overcome." (One of them began with the line, "Our feet are soaked.") They stopped every night, camping in giant tents. Rented trucks carried portable toilets. One minister, pursued to the toilet door by news photographers, yelled, "Can't a man even go to the john in peace?"

Although the march passed by segregationists, it also passed through small black towns where no one had ever been able to vote. An old woman came and kissed Dr. King, then ran off singing, "I done kissed the Martin Luther King!" Fifty people from one of those towns registered to vote for the first time after they saw the marchers.

The march passed Dexter Avenue Baptist Church and ended at the state capitol. King, who had left the march briefly to give a talk in Ohio, rejoined it at the end. George Wallace lurked inside the capitol, refusing to come out, and segregationists cursed and shouted. Yet at the rally on March 25, people sang, "We *have* overcome."

Jimmie Lee Jackson's grandfather said, "It was worth the boy's dying."

AMERICAN VOICES

❝ What do you want?"

"Freedom!"

"When do you want it?"

"Now! **❞**
—One of the common chants of the Civil Rights movement

What two deaths did the march end with?

The night the march ended, a white volunteer from Detroit, Viola Liuzzo, was shot and killed by Klansmen while driving black Civil Rights workers back to Selma.

According to a writer for *Ebony* magazine, the march also ended with the death of Jim Crow. It had taken the United States ninety-five years to enforce the Fifteenth Amendment, which said that "the rights of citizens of the United States to vote shall not be denied or abridged by the United States or by any state on account of race, color or previous condition of servitude."

Together the Civil Rights Act of 1964 and the Voting Rights Act of 1965 achieved the two main goals of the Civil Rights movement: Federal laws banned segregation in public places and protected black people's right to vote.

THE KINGS AT HOME

Martin Luther King had always said he didn't want to own property. But with four children (his youngest daughter, Bernice, was born in 1963), the family was outgrowing their small, rented house. Early in 1965 Coretta finally persuaded her husband they needed a house of their own. Even though the house they chose was quite simple, King still made all his friends tell him it wasn't too big or fancy.

Yoki would remember her mother as the one who "called the shots" because her father was away most of the time. It was Coretta who registered Yoki and Marty in a newly desegregated school in 1965. The day both Marty and Dexter had their tonsils out, Martin forgot to call to see how they were doing. Coretta watched him on TV that night, at the president's side as the Voting Rights Act of 1965 was signed. "In the end, I just had to get used to the fact that he would not be there," she said.

When King was home, he played baseball with his children but also taught them about his beliefs. They had to practice nonviolence. When other kids called Marty bad names, he wasn't allowed to call them names back. And when King saw his boys playing with some toy guns they had found, he told them that handguns were for hurting people. Marty and Dexter put their toy guns in a metal garbage can and burned them.

CHAPTER 7

"Where Do We Go from Here?"

Riots in Watts

Why did blacks riot in Watts?

As Malcolm X had said—and many young activists agreed—integration and voting rights would not help the poverty, anger, and hopelessness of many blacks, especially those living in northern cities. Less than a week after President Johnson signed the Voting Rights Act of 1965, a black Los Angeles ghetto called Watts exploded into a riot that lasted many days. The riots caused at least thirty-four deaths, one thousand injuries, and more than $40 million dollars' worth of property damage.

When King flew to Watts, people booed him. "We won," people told him. Looking at the ruins, King wondered *what* they had won. "We won because we made them pay attention to us," a young rioter told him.

Why did Martin Luther King bring the Civil Rights movement to Chicago?

King had been speaking about the need to address poverty, especially since he won the Nobel Peace Prize. He told Bayard Rustin that he had helped get African Americans the right to sit at a lunch counter and buy a hamburger, but that didn't help if they couldn't afford the hamburger. Poverty was causing blacks to riot in northern cities. There had been uprisings there before, but now they were becoming more and more common. The nonviolent movement was going up in flames—literally. King and the SCLC knew that they had to bring the movement to the North and show that nonviolence could address concerns other than voter registration and desegregation.

Chicago was the second-largest city in the U.S. and had more than a million black residents. Some people called it "the Birmingham of the North." Blacks were mostly poor, and they mainly had bad jobs or no jobs. Many lived in run-down, crumbling neighborhoods. Landlords didn't take care of the buildings, and the city didn't take care of the streets. And the people who lived there couldn't move out.

There weren't segregation laws—just agreements among neighbors, banks (which provided housing loans), and real estate companies that black people couldn't buy houses in "white" neighborhoods. "White" apartment buildings wouldn't rent to blacks either. And the run-down, dangerous apartments that blacks could rent were *more* expensive than nicer ones that they couldn't.

So, when Martin Luther King moved his family to Chicago in January 1966, he paid ninety dollars a month for a four-room apartment that was falling apart. (A much nicer, five-room apartment in a white neighborhood would have cost eighty dollars.) His neighborhood was called Lawndale, but there weren't any lawns. People called it "Slumdale."

What did King want to accomplish in Chicago?

King, the SCLC, and local black leaders called their mission the "Chicago Freedom Movement." King wanted Mayor Richard J. Daley to enforce laws that said landlords had to take care of buildings. He wanted fair housing practices to be enforced so that neighbors, banks, and real estate companies couldn't keep blacks out of certain neighborhoods. He also wanted companies to hire and promote blacks.

But there wasn't any easy way to do this. In Chicago, King's argument wasn't with stores or buses or even with laws. He couldn't boycott real estate companies. They could make plenty of money selling houses in white neighborhoods to white people.

Also, Mayor Daley was a clever politician. He showed King plans of how Chicago would get rid of its slums. He sent building inspectors to tell landlords to fix their buildings. (Someone, perhaps Daley, also arranged to fix up King's apartment. The local press joked that King could clean up the slums by moving from apartment to apartment.) But Mayor Daley wanted to be reelected, so he wasn't going to promise millions of dollars to build affordable housing. And he wasn't going to force white neighborhoods to integrate, because he feared riots.

The Chicago Freedom Movement didn't have any tools to change the city's problems. One of the movement's best tactics in the South had been to get television coverage of white violence against blacks. But showing the slums on TV wasn't going to help. Everyone could see the slums were terrible, but they couldn't see what caused them.

AMERICAN VOICES

❝ I'm not gonna beg the white man for anything I deserve. I'm gonna take it! ❞
—**Stokely Carmichael**, SNCC chairman, 1965

What event interrupted the Chicago Freedom Movement?

On June 6, 1966, student James Meredith was shot in the back and legs while marching across the state of Mississippi. Five years earlier the freedom riders had ridden buses across the South to test if waiting rooms were really desegregated. Meredith, the first black person to attend the University of Mississippi, wanted to test if the new Civil Rights acts made it possible for a black man to walk safely across his own state. They didn't.

Without delay, Martin and Coretta King (and their two older children), the SCLC, Stokely Carmichael (now the leader of SNCC), Floyd McKissick of CORE, and many others—black and white—went on a two-hundred-mile "James Meredith March Against Fear" across part of Mississippi. It was on this march that Carmichael began the chant that soon became a battle cry: "We want Black Power!" Carmichael also said that the Civil Rights movement should become all black (which SNCC did in 1966) and that violence should be met with violence.

King was worried. As usual, he was caught between the people who thought he was moving too slowly and the people who said that blacks should be satisfied with the Civil Rights and voting acts. Now he had to go back to Chicago and prove that nonviolence would work.

AMERICAN VOICES

❝Jingle bells, shotgun shells,

Freedom all the way.

Oh, what fun it is to blast

A trooper man away!❞
—SNCC tune sung on James Meredith March Against Fear, 1966

What happened to the Chicago movement?

On July 10, "Freedom Sunday," King addressed thirty thousand people in one-hundred-degree heat. He told people to boycott companies that failed to hire blacks for good jobs and to take their money out of banks that wouldn't loan blacks money. The crowd then marched to City Hall, where King imitated the man for whom he and his father were named. Just as Martin Luther had nailed a list of demands on a church door in 1517, Martin Luther King taped his to the metal door of City Hall. He called on the mayor to end discrimination, police brutality, and other acts that hurt black people. Daley wasn't there on Sunday, but when King handed him a copy of the demands on Monday, he was furious. He said Chicago already had anti-slum programs.

How do fire hydrants start riots?

The following Tuesday, some black kids turned on the fire hydrants to cool down, and when the police shut them off, several days of rioting began. "Rioting is the voice of the unheard," King had once said. He could understand this riot in a more personal way. He had seen what heat, bad smells, and no place to play did to the tempers of his own family. His children yelled and fought with one another that summer as they never had before.

During the riots King, Andrew Young, and the comedian Dick Gregory drove around talking to people in churches, on street corners, and in bars. After midnight John Doar·from the United States Justice Department showed up at King's apartment to see if he was all right. He could hardly believe his eyes. There was King, sitting on the floor explaining the theory of nonviolence to some of the most

violent young men in the city. King had packed his too small, too hot apartment with gang leaders. They were listening, too.

After several nights of bombings, gun battles, lootings, and fires, the governor, Otto Kerner, called in four thousand National Guardsmen. They patrolled the streets with Jeeps and machine guns in neighborhoods that looked like war zones. The rioting ended. A writer for the New York Times wrote that King's work with the gang leaders was as important as the arrival of the troops in ending the rioting.

On August 5 King led six hundred people, including white supporters, through a white neighborhood, with almost one thousand police there to protect them. Even the police were dodging bricks that were thrown. When King was knocked down by a rock that hit his head, the crowd yelled, "Nigger, go home!" Whites flipped over cars and set them on fire. King said, "I think the people from Mississippi ought to come to Chicago to learn how to hate."

Why did Martin Luther King's victory in Chicago feel like defeat?

The marches continued until Jesse Jackson, who was then a young member of the SCLC, planned a march through Cicero, a suburb where there had been riots in 1951. A young black man had just been murdered when he went there to apply for a job. King was in favor of the march, yet he was also concerned. The police and politicians were terrified. Cicero had seventy thousand people. There was no way even the police could prevent violence. Mayor Daley called King and agreed to all his demands. Everyone—including the banks and the real estate companies—would open the white neighborhoods to blacks, Daley said.

So King left the city, but Daley never kept the promises he had made. The movement's failure left the black residents of Chicago— and the nonviolent Civil Rights volunteers—bitter, angry, and tired. King came to a new conclusion: He was not going to persuade much of white America to agree that blacks were their equals. They had never intended to be fair to African Americans or to support integration. He was depressed. What could he do next?

To Seek out Strange New Worlds

In 1966 the black actress Nichelle Nichols (who played Lieutenant Uhura on *Star Trek*) was at an NAACP event. Someone told her that a fan wanted to meet her. That fan was Martin Luther King. He told her that *Star Trek* was one of the few shows that he and his wife liked their children to watch, because Lieutenant Uhura was the first black character in a position of authority in an integrated cast. She says that King told her, "People who don't look like us see us for the first time as we should be seen. As equals."

Where did King write *Where Do We Go from Here?*

In January 1967 he went alone to Jamaica, a Caribbean island, to think and to write. For two months he worked twelve to fourteen hours a day. He wrote about why blacks had to be proud. He said that while Black Power offered pride, he rejected its violence and its message of separation from whites. He said that blacks needed to use the freedoms they had while working for more. But he also said that blacks must join with poor whites, Mexican Americans, Puerto Ricans, and American Indians. Their fight was not against white people, he wrote, but against poverty and injustice.

Why did King begin speaking out against the war in Vietnam?

While King was still in Jamaica, James Bevel visited him and urged him to speak out against the war. King had seen the daily television broadcasts of the war—the first war America had fought since TV became popular. He saw burning villages and dead civilians. Many people in the United States believed that it was an unjust war. They believed that Americans shouldn't be trying to tell the Vietnamese whether or not to have a communist government. King agreed. Also, the war was very expensive. Money spent on planes and guns could be used to clean up the slums and pay for better schools.

It was also a war that was unfair to blacks and poor people. Young men had to sign up for the draft on their eighteenth birthdays, but men in college didn't have to fight. Even though blacks made up only 10 percent of the population, they made up 40 percent of the army. Poverty and bad schools made it hard for them to get good jobs and also made it difficult for them to go to college.

King began criticizing the war. He said that he could never again speak out against the oppression and violence that was directed at blacks unless he spoke out against the "greatest purveyor (supplier) of violence in the world today—my own government."

Were people pleased that King was speaking out against the war?

Many Americans were against the war and were glad to have a popular Civil Rights leader and Nobel Peace Prize winner on their side. Others felt that King had deserted the movement. Roy Wilkins of the NAACP, Jackie Robinson, *Life* magazine, and the *New York Times* said King was a good Civil Rights leader but he was just a preacher and should stay out of politics. J. Edgar Hoover said he had always known that King was a communist. And President Johnson was furious. He had delivered the Civil Rights acts and now King was speaking out against a war Johnson supported. That was the end of invitations to the White House for King.

In a speech on April 4, 1967, in New York City, King talked about how people responded to his antiwar messages. "Peace and Civil Rights don't mix," people had told him. But, he said, people who were surprised that he criticized the war didn't understand what he had been saying all these years. He had always been against *all* violence caused by racial conflict. His goal was not only to achieve justice, but peace as well.

Why did King come up with the idea for the "Poor People's Campaign"?

Riots were erupting in many American cities. It was a horrible time for King. Like many other times in his life, he felt he was expected to have all the answers—and he knew he didn't. Sometimes, Coretta Scott King wrote later, he said he just didn't want to talk to anyone because he didn't have anything to tell them. King ate too much and smoked too much (though never in public). He was depressed. When the *New York Times* printed a hostile editorial about an antiwar speech he had given, he cried.

In some ways this sounds like the young M.L. who jumped out a window when his grandmother died because he felt it was his fault. Andrew Young said King was feeling responsible for everything and guilty about everything. "He felt he should be able to wipe out poverty. He should be able to stop violence," Young remarked. King had spent twelve years trying to get African Americans the rights promised in the Constitution. Now he spoke of the need for entirely different values in society. He wanted a multibillion-dollar plan to rebuild the inner cities, a guaranteed income for everyone, and other changes in how wealth was distributed. Martin Luther King had become a revolutionary.

King proposed a "Poor People's Campaign" that would be sponsored by the SCLC. The poor of America would travel from all around the country and build a city of tents and shacks in Washington, D.C. Then the president and Congress would see the need for economic change.

What did the SCLC think of the Poor People's Campaign?

They thought that it was a bad idea. They thought the government would just say no, and they would look stupid. King said maybe they'd have to be in jail for a year or two. Young said he felt that King almost welcomed the idea of two years in jail, just so he could rest.

Still, plans for the campaign continued, and King traveled the country, listening to people's stories. Some lived in conditions as bad as in the days of slavery. One mother of six children lived on a plantation and earned only two dollars a day. The new Civil Rights voting laws had not solved the problems of justice in America, because they could not end poverty.

King didn't believe the Poor People's Campaign would bring economic equality, but he did believe it could be a demonstration of poverty that existed in a rich nation.

CHAPTER 8

A Committed Life

Martin Luther King Jr.,
speaking at a press conference

Why did King go to Memphis, Tennessee?

King's old friend and coworker James Lawson was now a minister in Memphis. He asked King to come speak to the black garbage collectors who were on strike. Some SCLC staff said King shouldn't get involved with the strike in the middle of his important Poor People's Campaign. King said that those men were exactly the people they were supposed to be helping. It was wrong that they earned "starvation wages in a rich nation."

On March 28, 1968, King led a march of the striking sanitation workers, but it was broken up almost immediately by young black men throwing rocks and breaking windows. King had always said he wouldn't lead a violent march, and so he left Memphis that night. Some men later told Andrew Young they had been paid to break up the march. It is possible that they were paid by the FBI.

Some of the news coverage said King had run away like "a scared rabbit." King saw this on TV while he and Coretta were having dinner with Ralph and Juanita Abernathy. He "looked like he was burning down," Juanita said. King went back to Memphis to plan a new march for April 5.

Why do some people believe King knew he was going to die on April 4?

Ralph Abernathy was supposed to speak at the mass meeting on April 3. It was a rainy night, and no one had expected many people to come. But more than two thousand people had showed up to hear Martin Luther King. When Young and Abernathy saw the crowds, they asked King to speak instead.

King was tired, but when he began to speak, he got caught up in his message. Although he was saying things he'd said before, he somehow seemed to forget how tired he felt. He was sweeping away his fears and everyone else's with the power of his words and voice.

King spoke of his death that night. He said, "I've been to the mountaintop. I've seen the Promised Land. I might not get there with you." But King had used that same language as far back as the Montgomery bus boycott. He had known since then that he might be killed at any time.

What was King doing right before his death?

On the afternoon of April 4, 1968, King was resting at the Lorraine Motel. Young and Lawson had come back from court, where they'd just gotten permission for the striking sanitation workers to march again. King threw a pillow at Young—then more pillows, and they had a pillow fight. Then someone knocked on the door to remind them that Reverend Samuel Kyles would be picking them up for dinner at his house. They all had to get up and change their clothes and act like grown-ups again.

When the Reverend Kyles arrived, King paused on the second-story balcony outside his motel room, trying to decide if he needed to get his coat. There was a noise like a firecracker. Abernathy looked onto the balcony. "Martin's lying down like we've been taught to when there's any shooting," he later said that he was thinking. Young thought that King was clowning around again. Then they realized King had been shot.

Coretta Scott King had heard about the shooting and started to the airport, but Martin was dead before she got there. She went back home to be with her children. Although a team of surgeons had worked to save King, he had a hole the size of a fist blown through his face and jaw.

Who killed Martin Luther King Jr.?

A white escaped convict named James Earl Ray was arrested and convicted of the shooting. Although Ray confessed, he soon said he was innocent. Some people, including members of the King family, believe the assassination was part of a conspiracy. The Kings got Ray a new trial, but he died in jail in 1998 of liver failure. In the 1999 court case, evidence showed that a man named Lloyd Jowers had paid someone—not Ray—to shoot King. The King family also believes that the FBI, CIA, and other organizations prevented a proper investigation of the assassination. The United States Justice Department says this isn't true. Other people believe that Ray was guilty but did not plan the murder alone.

It is hard to know the truth. It is true that the FBI interfered with the investigation of other Civil Rights killings and had a firm policy to "stop" King and his work. It is also hard to accept that a great man like King could have been killed so easily. Yet King and the people he worked with had always known this was not only possible, but likely.

What was King's funeral like?

Letters, phone calls, flowers, and gifts began pouring in as soon as King's death was announced. President Johnson and many other people called Coretta Scott King. Within a few days, around 150,000 people gathered in Atlanta, including President Kennedy's widow, Jacqueline; Robert Kennedy (who would be assassinated a few months later); future president Richard Nixon; and Vice President Hubert Humphrey.

For days King's body lay in an open casket so that people could walk past his coffin and say good-bye. Then he was taken to his boyhood church, Ebenezer Baptist, for the funeral. Nearly eight hundred people crowded inside; outside, thousands of people listened to the service on loudspeakers. It was bigger than any Civil Rights mass meeting.

Ralph Abernathy officiated at the funeral. Friends and family read from the Bible and from some of King's own sermons, and they sang hymns. The church service ended with King's own words, played from a tape of a sermon he had given at Ebenezer Baptist Church just two months earlier. He had spoken about how he wanted to be remembered when he died. He had asked that no one talk about his awards and honors, because they didn't matter. He said, "I'd like somebody to mention that day, that Martin Luther King Jr. tried to give his life serving others. . . . I won't have any money to leave behind. I just want to leave a committed life behind."

Martin Luther King would go on his "last great march," as Coretta called it. His coffin was carried on a farm cart pulled by two mules—a symbol of the Poor People's Campaign—halfway across Atlanta to the South View Cemetery. Thousands of people marched with him, walking past a hundred thousand other mourners, who cried or prayed as the coffin went by.

66 Dr. King's murder is a national disaster, depriving Negroes and whites alike of a leader of integrity, vision and restraint. 99

—Editorial in the *New York Times*

66 When white America killed Dr. King she declared war on us. . . . Get your guns. 99

—Stokely Carmichael

What happened after King's death?

Bayard Rustin said that one day he and King were talking about violent deaths of people such as Gandhi, who had dedicated their lives to nonviolence. King said that if he had to die like that, he hoped his death would be a symbol of the need for "justice, freedom, and peace" for all people.

Over the years this has been what many people remember about King, but at the time the response to his death was not peaceful. Riots broke out in more than one hundred cities after his assassination. The Black Power movement had already challenged the nonviolence movement.

Although the SCLC continued its work, it had been losing ground even when King was alive.

The Poor People's Campaign was still held in Washington that summer, but it did not change government policies.

Poor People's Campaign in June 1968

What is King's legacy?

Many people who lived through the Civil Rights movement say that it is hard to imagine how much the country changed. The changes—in segregation, in voting rights, in the election of blacks to public office, in the presence of blacks in jobs that were not open to them—are enormous. They are not only a result of King's work, but of the work of thousands of other people. Still, King did all that one man could do. His autopsy showed that although King died at thirty-nine, he had the heart of a sixty-year-old.

His family would never be free of his legacy. After King's death people asked Yolanda and Marty if they hated the man who had killed their father. They knew King would want them to forgive him, which is a hard thing to ask of a child whose father has just been assassinated. None of his children married or has children. His brother, A.D., was found drowned in his swimming pool eighteen months after Martin's death. An insane young man shot and killed King's mother as she played the organ in church one morning. And King's father died of a heart attack in 1984.

However, Christine King Farris and Coretta Scott King are both still living and have each written a book about Martin Luther King Jr.

King's birthplace and his house in Montgomery have become museums.

> **MARTIN LUTHER KING DAY**
>
> On November 3, 1983, President Ronald Reagan signed the bill that made the third Monday of every January a national holiday—Martin Luther King Jr. Day.

What would have happened if King had lived?

The Reverend Kyles, who was with King when he was shot, believes that if King had lived, his legacy would be quite different. He thinks there would be no Martin Luther King Jr. Day and no postage stamps with King's picture. The Civil Rights movement had already splintered. More and more people were disagreeing with him. At the March on Washington in 1963, King was preaching a dream of equality and brotherhood. By 1968 he was sounding nearly as revolutionary as J. Edgar Hoover claimed he was, demanding billions of dollars for guaranteed incomes for all people.

And yet, for countless people, he was beloved. Even when his movements failed, as in Albany, people held their heads up higher because they had been willing to defend their rights. Martin Luther King's family and friends said that he was no saint in his private life; King knew that too and wished he could have been a better person. He often worried about what to do next. Yet he spoke a message that transformed people and helped transform an era. It wasn't just *his* message, but he gave it a voice.

Martin Luther King told ordinary people—students, poor farmers, old women in church, the garbage men he was fighting for when he was killed—that they could change the country and the world.

And they did.

January 15, 1929 Born in Atlanta, Georgia

1944 Graduates from high school

1948 Graduates from Morehouse College and begins work at Crozer Theological Seminary

Ordained a Baptist minister

1951 Enters Boston University

1953 Marries Coretta Scott

1954 Moves to Montgomery, Alabama

The U.S. Supreme Court rules in *Brown v. Board of Education* that racial segregation in public schools is unconstitutional

1955 Receives Ph.D. from Boston University

Daughter Yolanda Denise King born November 17

Elected president of Montgomery Improvement Association (MIA)

November 13, 1956 Supreme Court rules that bus segregation is illegal

1957 Helps form Southern Christian Leadership Conference (SCLC)

Son Martin Luther King III born October 23

1958 Publishes *Stride Toward Freedom*; stabbed at book signing

Meets with President Eisenhower to discuss problems facing black Americans

1959 Travels to India

Resigns from Dexter Avenue Baptist Church in Montgomery

1960 Returns to Atlanta

Sit-in in Greensboro, North Carolina, launches sit-in movement

Arrested at sit-in

Student Nonviolent Coordinating Committee (SNCC) founded

President Eisenhower signs the Civil Rights Act of 1960 into law

1961 Son Dexter Scott King born, January 30

Congress of Racial Equality (CORE) begins first freedom ride through South

1962 Arrested during Albany movement

1963 Daughter Bernice Albertine King born March 28

Writes "Letter from Birmingham Jail"

August 28, 1963 March on Washington

Gives famous "I Have a Dream" speech

Sixteenth Street Baptist Church bombed

November 22, 1963 President Kennedy assassinated

1964 Honored as *Time* magazine's "Man of the Year"

President Johnson signs Civil Rights Act of 1964

Receives Nobel Peace Prize in Oslo, Norway

1965 Malcolm X assassinated in New York City

"Bloody Sunday" in Selma, Alabama

Selma to Montgomery March

President Johnson signs 1965 Voting Rights Act into law

1966 Moves into a Chicago slum

Begins working to end discrimination in housing, employment, and schools

James Meredith March Against Fear

1967 Speaks out publicly against the Vietnam War

Announces beginning of the Poor People's Campaign

Publishes *Where Do We Go from Here?*

1968 Marches in support of striking sanitation workers in Memphis, Tennessee

Delivers his last speech

April 4, 1968 Assassinated at the Lorraine Motel in Memphis

1983 National holiday created in King's honor

NONFICTION

Farris, Christine King. Illus. Chris Soentpiet. *My Brother Martin: A Sister Remembers Growing Up with the Reverend Dr. Martin Luther King, Jr.* New York: Simon & Schuster, 2003.

Levine, Ellen. Illus. Anne Rich. *If You Lived at the Time of Martin Luther King.* New York: Scholastic, 1990, 1994.

McKissick, Patricia, and Frederick McKissick. *The Civil Rights Movement in America from 1865 to the Present.* Chicago: Children's Press, 1987.

McWhorter, Diane. *A Dream of Freedom: The Civil Rights Movement from 1954 to 1968.* New York: Scholastic, 2004.

Myers, Walter Dean. *Malcolm X: By Any Means Necessary.* New York: Scholastic, 1993.

Patterson, Lillie. *Martin Luther King and the Freedom Movement.* New York: Facts on File, 1989.

FICTION

Crowe, Chris. *Mississippi Trial, 1955.* New York: Dial, 2002.

Curtis, Christopher Paul. *The Watsons Go to Birmingham—1963.* New York: Delacorte, 1995.

Moses, Sheila P. *The Legend of Buddy Bush.* New York: Simon & Schuster, 2004.

Taylor, Mildred D. *Mississippi Bridge.* New York: Dial, 1990.

Branch, Taylor. *Parting the Waters: America in the King Years, 1954–63*. New York: Simon & Schuster, 1988.

———. *Pillar of Fire: America in the King Years, 1963–65*. New York: Simon & Schuster, 1998.

Burns, Stewart. *To the Mountaintop: Martin Luther King's Sacred Mission to Save America, 1955–1968*. San Francisco: HarperSanFrancisco, 2004.

Dyson, Michael Eric. *I May Not Get There with You: The True Story of Martin Luther King, Jr.* New York: Free Press, 2000.

Frady, Marshall. *Martin Luther King, Jr.* New York: Viking Penguin, 2002.

Garrow, David. *Bearing the Cross: Martin Luther King, Jr., and the Southern Christian Leadership Conference*. New York: William Morrow, 1986.

King, Coretta Scott. *My Life with Dr. Martin Luther King, Jr.* New York: Holt, Rinehart, and Winston, 1969, rev. 1993.

Oates, Stephen. *Let the Trumpet Sound: A Life of Martin Luther King, Jr.* New York: HarperCollins, 1982.

Williams, Juan. *Eyes on the Prize: America's Civil Rights Years, 1954–1965*. New York: Penguin, 1987.

Wofford, Harris. *Of Kennedys and Kings: Making Sense of the Sixties*. New York: Farrar, Straus, Giroux, 1980.

140